S Mentoring for
Spiritual Growth

Published by
The Bible Reading Fellowship
15 The Chambers, Vineyard
Abingdon OX14 3FE
United Kingdom
Website: www.brf.org.uk

ISBN 978 1 84101 562 0
First published 2008
10 9 8 7 6 5 4 3 2 1 0
All rights reserved

Acknowledgments
Unless otherwise stated, scripture quotations taken from the *Holy Bible,
New International Version*, copyright © 1973, 1978, 1984 by International
Bible Society, are used by permission of Hodder & Stoughton, a division of
Hodder Headline Ltd. All rights reserved. 'NIV' is a registered trademark of
International Bible Society. UK trademark number 1448790.

Scripture quotations taken from The New Revised Standard Version of
the Bible, Anglicized Edition, copyright © 1989, 1995 by the Division of
Christian Education of the National Council of the Churches of Christ in
the USA, are used by permission. All rights reserved.

Scripture quotations from *THE MESSAGE*. Copyright © by Eugene H. Peterson
1993, 1994, 1995. Used by permission of NavPress Publishing Group.

A catalogue record for this book is available from the British Library

Printed in Singapore by Craft Print International Ltd

TONY HORSFALL

Mentoring for Spiritual Growth

Sharing the journey of faith

To my Renovare friends—Jonathan, Andy, Dave, Baz and Paul. How much I have appreciated your companionship and our days together!

Contents

⁜

Foreword

A recent report into the pressures faced by those in their twenties and thirties indicates that Christians in this age group are in need of great support in their development in the workplace, as believers and as leaders. But it's not only those people who need mentoring. If truth be known, we all need a mentor, whatever our age or responsibilities. I have personally been mentored by a Christian leader in the United States over recent years, and his support for me by phone, email or in person has helped me to gain clarity for the next phase of my life and ministry.

His name is Ben Campbell Johnson, and he is about 20 years older and 40 years wiser than me. When I stay at his lovely home in Atlanta he takes me on a morning jog. His advanced years and my lack of stamina mean this exercise regime gives us ample time to talk and to pray! Ben was for many years the Professor of Spirituality at Columbia Theological Seminary at Atlanta. With his understanding of the human spirit and his knowledge of Christian spirituality, these morning 'walks' are rich times of sharing.

He has challenged me to look for a deeper walk with Christ myself and to reflect on God's purposes for the next phase of my life and ministry. I believe that God looks for men and women like Ben who will disciple, coach and mentor other leaders, who in turn become leaders of leaders themselves.

To me, mentoring is essentially about relationship. It's a relationship in which a mentor helps a mentoree to reach his or her God-given potential. It's an experience in which one person empowers another person by sharing God-given resources, and it's a relational process in which a mentor, who knows or has experienced something, transfers resources of wisdom, information, experience, confidence or insight to a mentoree, thereby facilitating their development or empowerment.

I love the story of the mentoring relationship between Elijah and Elisha. Here we clearly see how wisdom from one generation is passed on to another. In 2 Kings 2:9 (NRSV) we read Elijah's offer to his protégé: 'Tell me what I may do for you before I am taken from you.' And Elisha replied, 'Please let me inherit a double share of your spirit.'

Similar examples can be found in Jesus' relationship with his disciples, in Barnabas' support for Paul and in Paul's mentorship of Timothy. Paul's exhortation to Timothy suggested that he wanted the process to continue. In 2 Timothy 2:2 (NRSV) we read: 'And what you have heard from me through many witnesses entrust to faithful people who will be able to teach others as well.'

Whether mentoring is intensive or occasional, there is much in this book to guide and stimulate the development of the relationship. And because mentoring is a great gift to the Church, let's use Tony's wise advice to make sure that it's done in the very best way possible!

Revd Dr Rob Frost
Director of Share Jesus International

✢

Introduction

This is a book about spiritual direction. It is a humble attempt to make this ancient Christian practice accessible and relevant to a new generation. For this reason I have chosen to use the term spiritual mentoring, since 'mentoring' is a word more commonly in use nowadays, and does not carry the same 'baggage' as a term like 'spiritual direction' does for some people.

I am aware that even the word 'mentoring' can be confusing, since it is used by different people in different ways, but it slots more easily into contemporary thinking and vocabulary and I have therefore preferred it. I am also aware that it is impossible to avoid using the term 'spiritual direction' altogether, especially when referring to the work of other writers, so at times the two will be used interchangeably.

Every book I have read in the last few years on the subject of spiritual direction has recognized in some way the startling growth of interest in this aspect of Christian ministry. It is a healthy and encouraging sign, for it shows a growing hunger to know God more deeply and a desire to take following Jesus seriously. It is happening all over the world, and among all types of church groupings. Everyone agrees that there is a need to understand the process of direction and to train others in its practice.

The rediscovery of this ministry is reflected in the increasing emphasis given to it by prominent Christian leaders. American writer and counsellor Larry Crabb, for example, has noted that in nearly 50 years of living as a Christian he has 'never seen the soul's thirst for God more talked about, more recognized as a vital motivation in the human personality or more strongly experienced as a consuming passion'. He goes on to say that 'nothing is more needed in advancing this revolution than making the idea of spiritual direction more biblically rooted and clearly understandable (insofar as mystery can be understood) and making the wise practice of spiritual direction more valued and common'.[1] Here in Britain, Selwyn Hughes began in the latter years of his life to introduce courses on spiritual direction into his training programmes. Two years before his death in 2006 he wrote this: 'I do not consider myself to be a prophet in the sense of foretelling events, but I believe that in the future spiritual direction is a practice that will be taken up by many in our evangelical churches.'[2]

Nor is it only the more reflective counsellors who are identifying and responding to this movement of God's Spirit. Some of the more active and outward-looking evangelists are responding to the same pull to inwardness. Leighton Ford, for many years an associate evangelist with Billy Graham, has described how, after a 30-year career preaching to large audiences all over the world, he took a sabbatical to find space and renewed vision. The time apart completely redirected his whole life, leading him to exchange the pulpit for the one-to-one ministry of spiritual direction.

British evangelist Rob Frost has also acknowledged the benefits of spiritual mentoring. Known for his dynamism and boundless enthusiasm, Frost has been behind many significant evangelistic efforts in Britain. Taking a retrospective look at his life and ministry, he recognizes that many of his struggles as a Christian would have been lessened if he had been mentored himself at an earlier stage. 'I'm convinced,' he says, 'that all Christians should see themselves as apprentices in the spiritual life and should seek guidance from those who have travelled further along the journey than they have. We all need spiritual directors who can navigate our hungry souls towards the feast of good things which God has prepared for us.'[3]

I am writing primarily (though not exclusively) for those in the evangelical and charismatic sections of the church. It is here that there has been most suspicion of the ministry of spiritual direction. It has to be said that there is a certain mystique surrounding the subject, which seems to take place in isolated monasteries or retreat houses, involve priests and nuns, and to employ language and practices that seem largely unfamiliar, if not a little suspicious. I hope this book will go some way to removing the mystery and the strangeness! Some, of course, fear that 'direction' may become authoritarian and are wary of any hint of sacerdotalism (the doctrine that ascribes special powers to ordained priests), given the close association it has with Roman Catholicism and 'high' Anglicanism. Others probably see no need for it, assuming that since we each have the Holy Spirit and the scriptures to guide us we can travel the Christian pathway without the need of external help.

As more and more evangelicals and charismatics are looking for a deeper experience of God, however, they are opening up to other traditions and finding the spiritual riches that are there; one example of these is the wisdom of having a 'soul friend' to help and advise. As they begin to experience contemporary examples of good practice in spiritual direction, they are realizing that it is not at all authoritarian and in fact highly rewarding. Increasing numbers are now enjoying the benefits of retreats and quiet days, and finding spiritual companions (to use another common term) to guide them on their journey of faith. Slowly the walls are being dismantled.

It seems to me that spiritual mentoring is ideally suited to meet the needs of an emerging generation of Christian men and women and the new crop of younger leaders. Postmodern culture is relationally oriented and resists the 'one size fits all' mentality of the previous generation. Pre-programmed discipleship packages are less likely to be effective as we move further into the 21st century. Mentoring offers the freedom to recognize that each individual is unique and that their story and journey are unique as well. Wisely practised, and because of its care for the nurture of the individual, it will liberate many into a deeper experience of God and a more radical discipleship. It is ideally suited to a context where many fresh expressions of church are blossoming. At its heart, spiritual mentoring is simply a relationship between two people for the purpose of spiritual growth. That is why one chapter in the book will be devoted to the more informal, and more common, ministry of what is often called spiritual friendship. Almost anyone can care for another as a 'soul friend', and part of my aim is to encourage members of local congregations to do just that for each other.

I also recognize that mentoring needs to be much more specialized than this as well, and I hope the text will help those who feel called to minister at a deeper level to prepare themselves for this much-needed and extremely worthwhile ministry. By definition mentoring is time-consuming and labour-intensive. We need to see many, many individuals called by God and equipped by the Spirit entering into this ministry if the hunger for God is to be satisfied and the church is to be strong enough to face the challenges of an increasingly hostile world.

I hope this book will be read by individuals who are already mentoring others or who are beginning to sense that God may be calling them in this way. I hope it will be read by church leaders to re-envision them about the real task of ministry. I hope it will be read in small groups, maybe by cell group leaders keen to see their members grow as much as they can in God, or by friends who meet together simply because they want to pursue God more intentionally. I hope it will be read by students preparing for ministry in local churches, helping them to see new possibilities for the shape of future ministry and by mission partners living and working in other cultures, needing to keep themselves spiritually fresh. Most importantly of all, I pray that it will be taken up in the hand of God and used by him to bring his people closer to him, thus making them more effective in their witness to the world.

✣

—————— *Chapter One* ——————

Point of departure:
What exactly is spiritual mentoring?

I was first introduced to the process of mentoring in 1999 by Rick Lewis, an Australian minister who came to Britain at the invitation of the Bible Society to introduce the idea to church leaders. I immediately responded with enthusiasm to what he shared, recognizing that mentoring was something I had already been doing instinctively for most of my life but also sensing that it would become a significant factor in shaping my future ministry.

Rick's definition of mentoring is very simple. Mentoring is promoting the work of God in the life of another. This simple definition resonated with something deep in my own heart as what I most wanted to do. I suppose it is linked with how God has 'shaped' me for ministry, but helping others to experience more of God registers very high on my scale of priorities and aims in ministry. Those who find themselves involved in spiritual mentoring usually say something similar, for it normally involves a call of God, a sense that this is what the Father wants us to do. This is one reason why we speak of 'spiritual' mentoring. It is not a technique or set of skills learned mechanically and used dispassionately. Spiritual mentoring is motivated by a sense of vocation or calling and energized by God.

Defining clearly the terms we use is important in any subject, for it means we have the same starting-off point, and this helps the clarity of our communication. Rick's definition got me started in thinking more carefully about mentoring, and since then I have come across a number of other definitions that have expanded my understanding of the term. It may be helpful to repeat here that I see mentoring as the basic skill of working in a one-to-one relationship with someone else so that the other person (let's call them the mentoree) can grow and develop in their faith. This means that mentoring is the 'hub' of many fairly similar activities. It can be used in a number of different directions—for pastoral care, for discipling, for coaching, for teaching, for counselling and for spiritual direction. I have used the term 'spiritual mentoring' to indicate that the skills of mentoring are being used in the process of spiritual direction. You may or may not agree with my use of the term in this way, but at least you will know what I mean by it!

As we look at each definition in turn we will see that they grow in complexity, and each adds something new to our overall appreciation of what is involved. As we ponder we will also try to ask three key questions about spiritual mentoring:

- Who is involved (people)?
- What actually happens (process)?
- What is it for (purpose)?

The first definition comes from the pen of Eugene Peterson, a much-respected writer and thinker based for many years at Regent's College in Vancouver. His writings have done much to open up evangelicals to the wider realm of Christian spirituality. He says, 'Spiritual direction takes place when two people agree to give their full attention to what God is doing in one (or both) of their lives and seek to respond in faith.'[1]

Here we see that normally spiritual mentoring involves *people* in a one-to-one relationship that is intentional and purposeful. This lifts it out of the informal, where a relationship might or might not develop, and puts it firmly into the formal category, where those involved are committed to the relationship. It has a definite *purpose* or goal in mind—understanding what God is doing in someone's life, and encouraging them to respond in some way to what is discovered through the sharing. In some cases, we note, this may be mutually beneficial. Further, the *process* requires some concentrated effort and is something we need to focus upon if it is to work. It demands our full attention.

Our second definition comes from John Mallison, a respected leader with Scripture Union in Australia. He is writing primarily about discipleship, which in my understanding is the process of helping believers become more established in the basics of the faith so that they can then live effectively for Christ and serve him fruitfully. His definition is sufficiently broad, however, to add to our appreciation of what is involved in spiritual mentoring: 'Christian mentoring is a dynamic, intentional relationship of trust in which one person enables another person to maximize the grace of God in their life and service.'[2]

Here we are reminded that we are using mentoring in a specifically Christian way. Again, it involves two people in a structured setting, but a new factor is introduced—the relationship is built upon trust. Mentoring depends upon friendship and the creation of a safe environment where it is easy to be open and vulnerable. A little more is disclosed to us about the *process*. It is an enabling relationship which results in empowerment for the mentoree, specifically helping the person to access the multi-faceted grace of God for themselves. The focus therefore is on God and the mentoree, not the mentor. The *purpose* is then to apply this to every aspect of life, and no aspect is considered to be outside the parameters of the mentoring relationship.

Bruce Demarest has worked among students in Europe and as a missionary in Africa and is presently a professor at Denver Seminary in the United States. He has written passionately about the need for evangelicals to engage more deeply with Christian spirituality and gives us this definition. Spiritual direction 'refers to the structured ministry in which a gifted and experienced Christian, called a spiritual director, helps another believer to grow in relationship and obedience to Christ.'[3]

Now we see something more about the *person* who offers direction. They are to be both experienced (in the ways of God) and gifted (by the Holy Spirit and through appropriate training). We will have more to say about the qualities of such people later in the book. The *process* is again said to need structure (agreement about when to meet, where, for how long and so on). A little more is said about the *purpose*, too. It is to bring about not only growth but obedience. This liberates the relationship from a cosy chat into a challenging exercise of discovering and doing the will of God.

Perhaps the writer who has most influenced my own thinking is Dr David Benner, a professor of psychology and spirituality based in Atlanta, Georgia. His own discovery of the importance of soul care and the value of a broader Christian spirituality has fired his passion for what he calls spiritual friendship. He writes:

Spiritual direction is a prayer process in which a person seeking help in cultivating a deeper personal relationship with God meets with another person for prayer and conversation that is focussed on increasing aware-ness of God in the midst of life's experiences and facilitating surrender to God's will. [4]

Now we are beginning to see why this is *spiritual* mentoring! When it comes to the *people* involved, the mentoree is passionately seek-ing a deeper relationship with God and comes to the relationship with a spiritual hunger, not looking for a quick fix but for help in finding ways to cultivate that relationship over a period of time. This means the relationship is growth-centred, not problem-oriented. This distinguishes it from counselling. The *process*, too, reflects a deeply spiritual approach that is soaked in prayer and that includes prayer as well as meaningful dialogue as key com-ponents. It involves seeking to identify the working of God in the events of everyday life, both the good and the bad, a process that requires discernment. Here the *purpose* is also spelt out in no un-certain terms: it is that the mentoree might give themselves fully to God's will for their life, whatever that might mean for them.

Our final definition is perhaps the most all-inclusive and comes from Keith Anderson and Randy Reese, two authors and spiritual mentors from the States. Here is their summary:

Spiritual mentoring is a triadic relationship between mentor, mentoree and the Holy Spirit, where the mentoree can discover, through the already present action of God, intimacy with God, ultimate identity as a child of God and a unique voice for kingdom responsibility.[5]

Now don't be afraid of the word 'triadic'—it has nothing to do with secret Chinese societies! It means that when it comes to the *people* involved, there are not just two but three—and the really important person is the Holy Spirit, who is the true spiritual director and the one on whom the whole relationship depends. This dependency on the work of the Holy Spirit is characteristic of most contemporary explanations of spiritual mentoring. When this is acknowledged and welcomed we need not be afraid of authoritarianism. The *process* is again seen as one of discernment, recognizing where God is already at work, but here the *purpose* is fleshed out in even greater detail.

We are introduced to three significant outcomes of the mentoring relationship. Firstly, the enjoyment of a closer relationship with God, based on his love for us, which matches the hunger that many people are feeling for a deeper connection with God. Secondly, and flowing out of the first point, the discovery of our true identity as God's beloved children based on who we are and not on what we do. This is liberating to busy Christians worn out by years of living on the treadmill of church activism. Thirdly, and flowing out of the first two, the recognition of what it is that God is calling us to do, and for what he has specifically gifted us.

The discovery of our unique 'shape' is then a natural outworking of his unconditional love for us and our secure identity as his children. This lifts Christian service out of the realm of drudgery and makes it an exciting and fulfilling adventure.

Can we now put this all together and form an overview of what we mean by spiritual mentoring?

The people: the mentor, probably a little further on in the Christian journey, seeks to establish a friendly relationship with the mentoree that encourages trust and provides a safe space for them to share their deepest desires, longings and fears. The mentoree comes to the relationship with a desire to grow spiritually, a hunger to know God more deeply, and a willingness to be open and vulnerable so that they may benefit from time with the mentor. The relationship may be informal but has normally a definite structure to it with clear boundaries and clear expectations on both sides. Crucially a third person is present throughout and is the true mentor—the Holy Spirit.

The process: it involves talking and sharing and assumes a listening attitude on the part of the mentor. No part of life is off limits as they explore together what is happening in the life of the mentoree and seek together to become more aware of what God is presently doing and saying in the circumstances of life. Both come in dependency on the Holy Spirit, seeking to attune themselves to his voice and discern together where he is leading.

The purpose: the mentoring relationship is an intentional one, for it has a clear aim in mind—to help the mentoree discover the all-sufficient grace of God and to apply this to their unique life situation and calling. It will inevitably involve at some stage the exploration of God's unconditional and personal love for them, the discovery of their unique gifts and calling, and the discerning of God's will for their future life and service. This does not happen overnight, of course, and so assumes an ongoing mentoring relationship over a period of time (although not necessarily an exclusive one).

Having grasped a little more clearly what we mean by spiritual mentoring, we can perhaps now see how it is different from some other aspects of soul care. Clearly there will be areas of overlap, and the different approaches blend together, but it is important to understand what is unique and distinctive about spiritual mentoring.

Spiritual mentoring is different from pastoral care for it goes beyond the needs of the present moment and deals with the bigger picture of life direction and purpose. It is different from discipling because it is concerned about the growth of the soul once a person is established in their faith. It is different from coaching in that it is not about teaching particular skills, but encourages the individual in the totality of their relationship with God. It is different from teaching because it is not so much about the impartation of knowledge as about the experience of God and the application of what we already know. It is different from counselling because it does not focus on problems but on potential.

David Benner describes spiritual mentoring as the 'jewel in the crown' of soul care,[6] and I wholeheartedly agree with his perspective. For me there is no greater joy or privilege than to promote the work of God in the life of another.

❖

Chapter Two

Ready for adventure:
The philosophy behind spiritual mentoring

Spiritual mentoring assumes a certain distinctive approach to the Christian life which may be new for some people. It involves a different way of looking at things, and in some cases will involve the adoption of a new mindset altogether. Rather than seeing spiritual formation as a static thing (which can be accomplished through set programmes and a rigid curriculum suited to all), it sees the way we become like Christ as a dynamic process that is never-ending. In some ways this process is both unpredictable and somewhat mysterious, since it is personal and unique to the individual. It is based on certain underlying assumptions which we will now begin to unpack.

The journey

The first assumption is that *the spiritual life is like a journey*. When we become believers we are only just starting out on what is a lifelong adventure. This contrasts sharply with some models of discipleship which give the impression that we have somehow 'arrived' when we come to faith. It contrasts, too, with those approaches that leave people high and dry after a heavy initial input in the first phases of discipleship, with nothing new to aim for, only more of the same. Spiritual mentoring assumes that there is always something more to learn, always something new to discover and always some new growth and development to take place.

The first call of Jesus to his disciples was 'Come, follow me' (Mark 1:17), an invitation at once simple in its content, yet far-reaching and challenging in its demands and implications. This Christ-following is a continual calling to follow in his steps (1 Peter 2:21), to walk as he walked (1 John 2:6), to respond to his leading (John 10:27) and to be where he is (John 12:26). We are called to follow Christ through the different stages of our lives. This journey through life has many phases to it: from birth through infancy to childhood; from childhood through the teenage years to adulthood; from adulthood through midlife to old age. Each stage is unique in its challenges and opportunities and demands its own response to following Christ. Jesus is relevant at every moment and at every turn on the road through life, and we need to develop a spirituality that is appropriate for where we are on life's journey. Spiritual mentors can help us navigate our way through the various transitions of the years, enjoy and appreciate the different 'seasons' and negotiate safely both the mountain tops and the deepest valleys that will inevitable form part of our journey.

We are called to follow Christ in becoming like him in our thoughts, words, character and actions. This has been called the transformational or inner journey, and it reminds us that as we travel through life we are meant to change. The goal is that Christ be formed in us, so that we become imitators of him, not in some external sense of copying a detached standard, but in the sense of allowing the Christ who dwells within us to express himself through us (Galatians 4:19; Colossians 1:27). Spiritual mentoring provides a safe place where we can explore how God is at work to make this transformation a reality in our lives. It presents us with enough encouragement to keep pressing on and sufficient challenge to avoid complacency or inertia. We are called to follow Christ, too, in living for him day by day and in serving his cause in the world. This may mean following in a geographical sense wherever he may lead us, either in our own country or elsewhere. Like Abraham, we may well find we are called to leave our own country and go to a place that God will show us (Hebrews 11:8). Implicit in the call to 'follow' is for some a command to 'go' as well (John 15:16).

It may involve finding a place of service within our church or local community, discovering our spiritual gifts and then selflessly using them for the benefit of others. However the call to serve Christ works itself out, it will require obedience, and an ongoing obedience at that. Just as Israel were led by the movement of the cloud by day and the pillar of fire by night, so we will find that when we settle down God will again stir our hearts to lead us into some new expression of following (Exodus 13:20–22). Sometimes guidance will be clear and simple; at other times it may be difficult to discern the right thing to do. Spiritual mentors can offer us help at such moments of decision.

One thing I admire about the apostle Paul is that he was always reaching out after God, never stagnant in his pursuit of the One who had called him. No complacency entered his soul, causing him to adopt a 'cruise control' mode. Rather, the path still stretched ahead of him, and with undiminished enthusiasm he set himself to follow his Master. 'Not that I have already obtained all this or have already been made perfect,' he said, 'but I press on to take hold of that for which Christ Jesus took hold of me. Brothers, I do not consider myself yet to have taken hold of it. But one thing I do: Forgetting what is behind and straining forward towards what is ahead, I press on towards the goal to win the prize for which God has called me heavenwards in Christ Jesus' (Philippians 3:12–14).

The inner life

The second assumption that lies behind spiritual mentoring is the belief that *the inner life sustains the outer life*. In a fast-paced culture, alive with high-speed technology and bursting with opportunities for involvement, it is easy to fall into the trap of thinking that the external world of activity is all that there is. Spiritually minded people, however, know that the real action takes place in the unseen realm in which prayer is offered, faith is exercised and God is at work. The process of spiritual mentoring gently calls us back to the truth that the inner life needs to be acknowledged, strengthened and cared for.

A tree cannot grow upwards and produce fruit unless it first grows downwards and is nourished and supported by a healthy root system, which is hidden from view. Taller trees need deeper roots; without them they will be blown over when the storms come. Likewise, the more we are involved in the busyness of daily life, even if it is in service to others, the more we need to care for our own inner selves. This is why spiritual mentoring often takes place in the context of retreats or quiet days. This gives us permission to slow down and provides a setting of stillness and an opportunity to reflect and think more deeply about what is happening to us, where we are going, and whether we are living in accordance with our true values. It says in Proverbs 4:23, 'Above all else, guard your heart, for it is the wellspring of life'.

Spiritual mentors will therefore challenge us to develop a balance in our lives between work and rest, activity and intimacy. They will remind us that our true identity does not lie in our performance or our productivity, but in the fact that we are God's beloved children and that we do not need to earn or maintain his favour by what we do. They will help us to let our being become the ground of our doing, and to work from a place of spiritual rest, where we know our acceptance with God is secure and not dependent on what we do or don't do, and where we minister out of a true awareness of who we are, not from an image we project. For me personally, the discovery of my own belovedness has been one of the great blessings of my Christian life, transforming my relationship with God and the way I serve him.

In no way do spiritual mentors wish to take the place of God in our lives. Indeed, their objective is to encourage us to hear God for ourselves. They minister under the terms of a new covenant, with the knowledge that every child of God can hear the voice of God for themselves (Hebrews 8:11). By calling us back to the nurture of the inner life, they provide a setting that makes it easier for us to hear the still small voice of God and to notice the subtle movements within our souls. They help us to train our hearts to recognize the whisper of divine love, and they challenge us continually with the question, 'And what is God saying to you?' In the rush of each day and the hurly-burly of our response to need we may miss out on hearing the life-giving voice of God unless we truly listen.

God's presence

The third underlying assumption is that God is *always present and acting in our lives*. The God of grace is always the first mover, taking the initiative and reaching out towards us. Our responsibility is to recognize what he is doing and to respond with faith and obedience. We all realize how difficult this can be. We become so wrapped up in our own affairs, so caught up with the present moment and so absorbed in ourselves that we often fail to recognize when God is around us. It has always surprised me that despite the noise of angelic choirs and the appearance of supernatural stars in the night sky, most people in Bethlehem were oblivious to the birth of the Messiah. The most important event in history simply passed them by. How much of God's activity do we miss by our preoccupation with our busy little concerns?

Spiritual mentors invite us to recognize that God is always present in the world, and they work with us to help us discern his footprints. They agree with the ancient poet, quoted by the apostle Paul, who said, 'For in him we live and move and have our being' (Acts 17:28). We live in a God-filled world and our job is to awaken to his presence, notice what he is doing, and go with the flow of divine activity. Consequently, the work of the mentor, as Anderson and Reese point out, is 'not to create but to notice, not to invent but to discern'.[1]

This process of co-discernment is integral to the mentoring process. God is present in the circumstances of our lives, and his word is already written in our personal stories. By providing an objective presence, spiritual mentors enable us to recognize how God has been at work in the past, is currently at work in the present, and where this might lead us in the future. By encouraging us to look for God in everything, and opening our eyes to his presence all around us, they awaken us to the joyful possibility of living more consciously in the awareness of his closeness. There is no place where he is not. Every place can be a sacred place if we have eyes to see.

According to David Benner, this attentiveness to God's presence, and our experience of that presence, is at the heart of spiritual direction. He quite rightly states that 'the master goal of spiritual direction can therefore be described as *the facilitation of this attunement to God's presence*' (his italics).[2] In the light of this, it is easy to see why spiritual mentoring can be described as a prayer process or, as someone has put it, 'holy listening'. Both mentor and mentoree are seeking to tune in to God, to have 'ears to hear' what the Spirit is saying.

Here then is the background to spiritual mentoring. It sees the Christian life as an adventure, an exciting journey with God. It invites us to value and appreciate the inner life and to learn to live from within, from our hearts. It recognizes the presence of God in every part of life and trains us to come alive to his voice and respond to his activity.

Considering the benefits that spiritual mentoring can offer, it is not surprising that increasing numbers of people are looking to find their own companion on the journey. Some are drawn through the longing of their own hearts to know God more deeply. Some come because they feel confused and bewildered and want to make sense of what is happening to them. Others recognize the danger of burnout, are aware they need help to live in a more balanced way and want to learn how to serve God more efficiently and effectively in the rhythm of his grace.

Howard Baker was actively involved in youth ministry, energetically throwing himself into his work and committed to it one hundred per cent. Then one day, out of the blue, he woke up to the cold reality of his inner life. He realized he felt frustrated and angry at the meagre results he was seeing for all his hard work. He began to admit that he was afraid of close relationships and that much of his motivation for service was his need to be successful and appreciated. The painful awareness dawned on him that he had lost his spiritual fire, and that he had lost his soul to the chief rival of true devotion to Jesus—Christian activity. Worse still, he felt he did not know how to change things or to develop a strong inner life. 'So here I was,' he wrote, 'a Christian man, a guy working in Christian service, faced with a growing deadness inside.'[3]

Baker's willingness to be honest with himself and face the numbness he felt inside led him to explore spiritual direction. It opened him up to some of the ancient paths of soul care, and eventually restored his passion for living and for God: 'I discovered the benefits of allowing a spiritual director to take an honest look at my soul with me and direct me into the presence of God. I felt as if I might really be rejoining God on the path he had laid out for my life.'

Baker's story and testimony have been echoed by many others. Perhaps you feel now as he did then. So why not do as he did and consider finding a spiritual mentor? Why journey alone, when there are others to guide you and to travel with you? Or, if you have been helped yourself, why not consider using your experience to help others?

─────── *Chapter Three* ───────

Ancient paths:
Spiritual mentoring in the Bible
and Church history

It had been a long day for a young man, and since early dawn Samuel had been busily attending to his duties within the temple courts with the conscientiousness for which others admired him. Now as the evening came, and with the last of his jobs safely taken care of, he was ready to lie down and rest. Most nights he fell asleep as soon as he lay down, so worn out was he by his day's work. This night, however, he was restless in a strange kind of way, and sleep would not come.

Still in that half awake, half asleep stage, he thought he heard a voice. He assumed it was the priest, Eli, an old man now and prone to forget things. 'What is it now?' thought Samuel as he tiptoed across the cold temple floor to where the old man was sleeping. To his surprise the elderly priest denied having called him, so Samuel returned to his bed and once more waited impatiently for sleep to come. Then, a second time he heard his name. Surely it was Eli calling him! Again a second time he got up and stood before the priest, only to find the same response. Eli had not called him, yet he was sure someone had.

Samuel repeated the ritual of getting back into bed and trying to sleep, but to his annoyance and surprise, the voice came again, calling him by name. This time he was sure it must be the old man. Impatiently he approached Eli a third time. 'You did call me,' he said and waited shivering to be told what to do. The old man paused and said nothing for a moment, then sat up on the bed as if he had something important to say: 'Go and lie down, and if he calls you, say, "Speak, Lord, for your servant is listening."'

This little incident, recounted for us in 1 Samuel 3:1–9, is a classic and early example of spiritual mentoring. Mentoring is neither the latest fad nor is it something recently invented. It has been around for a long time, and what we are seeing today is not the discovery of something new, but rather a rediscovery of an ancient spiritual practice which has sadly been ignored by some sections of the church.

Samuel, we are told, did not yet know the Lord in a mature sense and was not yet skilled in recognizing the voice of God for himself (v. 7). He needed the help of someone a little further on in the journey of faith to help him recognize the movement of God in his life. Eli, for all his weaknesses and shortcomings, was something of a father in the faith to the young lad, and although he was also a little slow himself to catch on (remember that 'the word of the Lord was rare' in those days: v. 1), he eventually did recognize that it was God who was calling the boy. With remarkable wisdom he sends Samuel to lie down and rest, knowing that if it is indeed God calling, he will speak again. He also advises Samuel as to how to respond when the time comes.

Those from an evangelical background will particularly need reassurance that spiritual mentoring is biblical—that it is both sanctioned and illustrated by scripture. In fact we can see the process at work in the interactions between many Old Testament characters—for example, Jethro and Moses, Moses and Joshua, Elijah and Elisha. I think we see it in embryonic form in the ministry of the 'seers', that unusual group of individuals who were a cross between prophets and priests and to whom individuals like King David looked for guidance (1 Samuel 9:8–10; 2 Samuel 24:11). I would suggest, too, that the ministry of the high priest, who was able to 'deal gently with those who are ignorant and are going astray, since he himself is subject to weakness' (Hebrews 5:2), in some ways anticipates the ministry of soul care that we are describing.

When it comes to the Gospels, we need look no further than to the example of Jesus. Indeed, Jesus is the model spiritual director who provides us with both a pattern for spiritual guidance and an illustration of the qualities of an ideal spiritual mentor. 'Virtually every conversation Jesus had and every teaching he gave offered spiritual guidance,' Bruce Demarest writes. 'He focussed on primary issues of knowing, being and doing—constantly directing people to right beliefs, right relationships, and right conduct.'[1] We have only to consider how Jesus spoke to the Samaritan woman (John 4:1–26), reflect on the way he responded to the woman caught in adultery (John 8:1–11), or notice how he dealt with the rich young ruler (Luke 18:18–25) to conclude that this is probably an accurate assessment.

A closer look at the way Jesus worked with Peter illustrates the benefits of an ongoing mentoring relationship. From the moment of the initial call to discipleship, Jesus saw the potential within the person regarded by many as a 'rough diamond'. He changed his name from Simon to Peter, meaning 'rock' (John 1:42). This is the one clear message that all mentors should communicate to those they seek to help: 'I believe in you.' Often Jesus would visit Peter's home and their friendship grew and developed naturally over time (Mark 1:29–30). Jesus shared his life with all the disciples, teaching by example and allowing them to get to know him better. Peter was part of the inner group of three (with James and John) who were especially close to the Master. Patiently Jesus answered Peter's many questions, explained matters that were unclear and gently corrected his mistakes and misunderstandings. He provided opportunities for Peter's faith to grow, and debriefed him on the lessons he was learning (Luke 5:1–11). At times Jesus used leading questions to help Peter articulate what he was coming to understand (Matthew 16:15–16) and when he saw the growth taking place within him, he was not afraid to put responsibility and leadership into his hands

(Matthew 16:17–18). Sometimes Jesus would have to curb Peter's natural enthusiasm (Matthew 17:1–9; John 18:10–11), warn him to guard against his weaknesses (Matthew 26:33–35) and forgive his failures (Mark 14:37–38). Throughout the process Jesus remained loyal and committed to this wholehearted follower, demonstrating the unconditional nature of his love. Perhaps the skill of Jesus as a mentor is best seen in the way he lovingly restores Peter to faith after his denial and wisely points him back to the call upon his life. Through a series of penetrating questions Jesus not only gets Peter to relive the past and learn from his mistakes but also challenges him afresh to fulfil his calling to care for God's people (John 21:15–19). The whole dialogue recorded by John is a wonderful example of spiritual mentoring at its best.

Jesus, then, gives us our best example of what it means to be a mentor, and how to go about it. He makes himself available to people, deals with them as unique individuals and engages them in creative dialogue. He listens carefully and asks penetrating questions, affirming and encouraging them on their spiritual journey. Skilfully he applies the word of God to their lives, helps them to identify and remove obstacles to growth and patiently bears with them in their mistakes and failures. Throughout he remains committed to them in love.

Beyond the Gospels we can see that the first believers continue the practice of soul care towards each other. Paul had himself sat at the feet of Gamaliel and was accustomed to learning from wiser people (Acts 22:3). He maintained a special relationship with the churches he founded, regarding himself as their 'father' in the faith, and many of his letters are examples of the spiritual mentoring of whole congregations. (Letter-writing, or nowadays email, has always been a good way of mentoring from a distance.) At the same time he recognized the existence of 'guides' or 'guardians' who also contributed to the growth of God's church and God's people. Such people he expects to be present in abundance ('ten thousand'; see 1 Corinthians 4:15). We often read in the Gospels of 'blind guides' like the Pharisees, and Paul warns us against those who set them-selves up as guides but whose lives do not match up with their calling (Matthew 23:16; Romans 2:17–21). Nevertheless the need for genuine mentors remains. The word Paul uses in 1 Corinthians 4:15 is the word *paidagogos* which means a trainer or instructor. In contemporary society the *paidagogos* was entrusted with the responsibility of training young boys and guiding them into man-hood and maturity. Whilst the Holy Spirit remains the principal mentor of God's people (John 16:13), we all need other people to come alongside us and help us make progress spiritually, as the Ethiopian discovered when he met Philip (Acts 8:30–31).

Paul's philosophy of ministry was securely built around the principle of mentoring others. He writes to Timothy: 'You then, my son, be strong in the grace that is in Christ Jesus. And the things you have heard me say in the presence of many witnesses entrust to reliable people who will also be qualified to teach others' (2 Timothy 2:1–2). Paul was especially gifted at gathering around him groups of people, both men and women, in whom he saw potential and whom he nurtured in the faith. Clearly he regarded Timothy in a very special way. Having met the young man on one of his missionary journeys, he was delighted to take him with him as they travelled on, and to invest time and energy into his spiritual growth. Timothy appears to have done many 'errands' for the apostle and visited many of the newly established churches in the Medi-terranean lands before settling down at Ephesus to lead the church there.

The two epistles written by Paul to Timothy are really his spiritual counsel to the young leader. They remain an invaluable source of spiritual wisdom for anyone in church leadership anywhere in the world at any time. Paul reminds Timothy of the very genuine love that he has for him and assures him of his prayerful support, while exhorting him not to be afraid but to depend on the power of the Spirit (2 Timothy 1:1–7). Aware of Timothy's personality, Paul urges him to be strong and to remember his calling, to draw strength from what the Lord said to him at that time, and not to flinch in the spiritual battle (1 Timothy 1:18; 6:12; 2 Timothy 2:1–2). Recognizing his youthfulness, he should not feel inferior because of his age (1 Timothy 4:12) but should avoid the particular temptations that might come because of it (2 Timothy 2:22), and at the same time set a positive example for others. Bearing in mind his physical weakness, he is to look after himself and his health (1 Timothy 4:8; 5:23). Paul encourages Timothy to excellence in all he does (1 Timothy 6:11; 2 Timothy 2:15), especially in the development of his gift of preaching and teaching (1 Timothy 4:13–14; 2 Timothy 3:14–17; 4:2). There will be opposition and even suffering, so Timothy should safeguard the message of the gospel and remain steady in all circumstances (1 Timothy 6:20; 2 Timothy 4:5). While a letter hardly involves a dialogue, there is a flow of warmth from Paul and an expression of personal vulnerability as the apostle shares his own loneliness and sense of disappointment in ministry (2 Timothy 4:6–18). He longs to see Timothy again, for this mentoring relationship gives blessing both ways (2 Timothy 4:9, 21). Finally, Timothy is asked to do the spiritual work of reflection so that he can benefit fully from this counsel (2 Timothy 2:7).

There is therefore plenty of biblical precedent and encouragement for the ministry of spiritual mentoring. Not surprisingly, the history of the church is full of examples of this being put into practice. Of course, a different terminology is often used, and it is not always as clearly defined as we have made it, but it is there like a silver thread running through the history of God's people.

We probably see it first in the Desert Fathers, those who went out into the wild and lonely places to engage in spiritual warfare and to seek God more intently. Men like Anthony of Egypt and John Cassian attracted many spiritual followers who valued their wise sayings and counsel. With the advent of monastic communities, abbots like Benedict gave spiritual guidance to their orders through the establishment of a rule of life, while the Celtic Christians of the fifth and sixth centuries encouraged believers to find a soul friend (*anam cara* in Gaelic). It was Brigid of Kildare who famously said, 'Anyone without a soul friend is like a body without a head.'

Into the Middle Ages and we find Bernard of Clairvaux writing hundreds of letters of spiritual guidance, and Aelred of Rievaulx with his book on spiritual friendship, in which we read these beautiful words: 'Here we are, you and I, and I hope a third, Christ, is in our midst… Come now, beloved, and open your heart, and pour into these friendly ears whatsoever you will, and let us accept gracefully the boon of this place, time and leisure.'[2]

During the Reformation, Martin Luther published his *Letters of Spiritual Counsel* and John Calvin, often described as the 'Director of Souls', also wrote many letters to care for the spiritual needs of those under his charge. At a similar time, during what is known as the Counter-Reformation, we see the flowering of a deep spirituality within the Roman Catholic Church. Ignatius of Loyola is probably the founder of the modern retreat movement, and his famous Spiritual Exercises are the basis for many who lead such times today. During the same period we also encounter Teresa of Avila, one of the first to map out the stages of growth in the spiritual life in her book *Interior Castle*. Her contemporary, John of the Cross, developed through his mystical poetry an understanding of what is often called 'the dark night of the soul', that experience when God seems to have abandoned us but is in fact drawing us even closer to himself. His words have guided many since to find peace in the midst of darkness.

Seventeenth-century Puritan preachers and pastors such as Richard Sibbes and Thomas Goodwin were also concerned with spiritual growth. John Bunyan wrote his famous book *The Pilgrim's Progress*, which so wonderfully describes the Christian journey. Richard Baxter wrote two influential books, *The Reformed Pastor* and *The Soul's Everlasting Rest,* both of which begin to describe the growth and care of the soul. In the 18th century John Wesley intro-duced the class system to nurture those converted during the revival, which came to Britain during his ministry. The class system was essentially an exercise in group spiritual direction, as it called individuals to meet together regularly and give an account of their growth in God and seek for greater personal holiness.

More recently there have been other men and women of God who have encouraged, as much by their writings as anything, the tradition of spiritual counsel. Andrew Murray, the South African minister, impacted many through his books (for example, *Abide in Christ* and *The True Vine*) and his clear call to a deeper inner life. C.S. Lewis was a mentor to many through his letters and wise counsel, as well as to a whole nation through his regular radio broadcasts and his many books, which continue to sell across the world. Thomas Merton continues to have a wide influence through his writings 40 years after this death; the Roman Catholic priest, Henri Nouwen has also written many books, which are read widely. Among Protestants, writers like A.W. Tozer kept the flame of true spirituality burning brightly, and more recently Richard Foster, Joyce Huggett and Dallas Willard have reminded evangelicals of the benefits of nurturing the soul and the value of spiritual disciplines, in particular spiritual direction.

It is clear, then, that spiritual mentoring had always been around, and we need not be suspicious of it! Dallas Willard summarizes the position succinctly: 'Spiritual direction was understood by Jesus, taught by Paul, obeyed by the early church, followed with excesses by the medieval church, narrowed by the Reformers, recaptured by the Puritans, and virtually lost in the modern church.'[3] What we are seeing now is a remarkable resurgence of interest in this whole area, which can only be the work of God. It is the Holy Spirit, the true spiritual guide, who is calling the church back to one of its most ancient paths.

——— *Chapter Four* ———

Travelling companions:
What it means to be a spiritual friend

I do a lot of travelling for my work, mostly on my own, which I usually don't mind because it gives me time and space to think and reflect. However, if I'm on a long journey, maybe involving air travel and visiting a new country, I would certainly prefer to have a travelling companion with me—someone to talk with and pass the time, someone to be there in delays or hold-ups or scary moments, someone to share the fun and adventure of the trip. There is definitely something about a shared journey that makes travelling a whole lot easier.

Those who find the term 'spiritual direction' difficult often substitute it with the term 'accompaniment', which puts across the idea of sharing the spiritual journey together, of being travelling companions. Another term often used is that of 'spiritual friendship', which again softens what can appear to be a somewhat harsh term, and reminds us that friendship is at the heart of any mentoring relationship. Spiritual friends are those who accompany us on our spiritual journey, who come alongside us in our moments of need and help us to keep on track, making our journey easier and less lonely. In this sense the terms 'spiritual mentor' and 'spiritual friend' are very similar and may be used interchangeably.

Most of us probably have a network of friends, acquaintances, colleagues and contacts, but in truth we probably do not have many deep relationships. It takes a lot of time to develop meaningful friendships and a lot of grace to sustain them over the years.

Happy the man or woman who manages to find another person with whom they can share openly and honestly from the depth of their being!

The Bible is full of examples of good friendship, people whom we could describe as being 'soul friends'. One example is that of David and Jonathan and the brotherly love they shared (1 Samuel 18:1–4). They were truly kindred spirits and committed themselves to each other in covenant, despite the difficulty of maintaining their relationship in the face of King Saul's hatred of David. It was a friendship that sustained and encouraged them both. Then there were Ruth and Naomi (Ruth 1—4). They stood by each other despite their many adversities and encouraged each other to keep trusting God when their situation was very bleak. It was a mutually beneficial relationship, for when one was weak the other was strong and vice versa. Think, too, of Mary and her older cousin, Elizabeth (Luke 1:39–45). When the reality of all that is going to happen dawns on Mary, she cannot wait to share her story with someone else whom she can trust and who will understand. She hurries to Elizabeth's home because she knows that there she will find welcome, acceptance, a listening ear and some good advice. And where would the apostle Paul have been, had not his good friend Barnabas taken him under his wing, and gone in search of him when he might have given up (Acts 9:27; 11:25–26)? What a wonderful example of a spiritual friend Barnabas is, investing time in the new convert, believing in him when others doubted, helping him to grow in the faith, and then humbly standing aside as his protégé's greater gifts came into play.

Spiritual friendship can operate on two different levels. It can work as an informal relationship between friends, perhaps members of the same church or colleagues in the same missionary team or just people who live near each other. They relate primarily out of their love and respect for each other and in a peer relationship— they are on an equal footing, with a high degree of mutuality, of give and take. They are likely to meet frequently and see each other socially as well. For the sake of clarity we might reserve the description 'soul friends' for this level of soul care.

Spiritual friendship can also operate on a more formal level when there is a need for a degree of expertise. It may be that a person is drawn to someone who is further down the spiritual pathway and desires to learn from them because they see something in that person they would like to build into their own walk with God; or they may just feel the need of guidance from someone who is outside their situation and who can give an objective perspective. This kind of relationship will be friendly, but probably not have a social dimension. It will not be based so much on give and take, since one person has to provide the objectivity and expertise the other needs. It may well involve a greater physical distance between the two people, and meetings will be less frequent but more planned and purposeful. We might call this 'spiritual mentoring' in its wider sense.

With that slight distinction in our minds, we can now ask what spiritual friendship involves. No matter at which level we choose to operate, spiritual friendship involves four component parts. Spiritual friends (or mentors) provide a safe place; they lend a listening ear; they offer wise counsel; and they give continuing support.

Spiritual friends (mentors) provide a safe place

'Hospitality' is a word that is often used in this context. It doesn't mean providing food and drink (although a cup of coffee is often appreciated!), but providing space in our lives to allow people to feel at home and relaxed. Time is in short supply for most people, so the gift of quality time together (say an hour or so) is something to be really appreciated. It makes the mentoree feel valued and respected.

We have seen already that a mentoring relationship works on the basis of trust. The mentoree must feel that this is a safe place where what they have to share will be taken seriously, without ridicule, shock, judgment or criticism. They must also know that what they say will not be passed on to others; confidentiality is vital in establishing trust. Trust is difficult to create, but easy to lose. It may be there because of an existing relationship, or it may have to be built over a period of time. It cannot be hurried; it has to be earned. Bryn Hughes says that trustworthiness is based upon certain personal characteristics such as consistency, integrity, supportiveness, reliability and competence. He also notes how vitally important trust is in mentoring relationships. He says: 'It's the oxygen of human relationships at all levels, including marriages, families and churches, so it is critical that folk who seek to disciple others earn and understand trust. Every mentoring relationship has a plateau that is determined by the level of mutual trust.'[1]

The safe place we seek to offer is a place of grace. As people realize they can trust us, so they will begin to open up to us and reveal their true story. This is an enormous privilege, and as they take the risky step of revealing themselves, we must meet them with a response of grace. This means accepting them for who they are, and accepting them at whatever stage they are on their journey. Only when people face their true selves and meet with grace can they discover their identity as God's beloved children. Generally speaking, people open up layer upon layer. Each successful peeling away of defensive covering leads to greater freedom and a willingness to be even more vulnerable. David Benner's penetrating words underline the importance of creating a context for grace: 'The most important thing I can do is help the other person be in contact with the gracious presence of Christ. If I bring anything of value to the meeting, it is that I mediate divine grace.'[2]

Spiritual friends (mentors) lend a listening ear

I have noticed on the retreats I lead that whenever we offer an opportunity to listen to individuals, the slots are taken up straight away, almost with a rush! It shows the great hunger we have to be truly listened to and the aching need in many hearts to be able to share at a deep level. I am continually amazed and humbled at what people reveal, even in a half-hour slot.

I used to think that I was a good listener. I assumed that because I was in pastoral work and enjoyed it when people shared their stories with me, I could listen well. It was when I attended a training course on listening skills that I realized my listening often amounted to waiting for my turn to speak or running ahead of the person and making assumptions about what they were saying. I had to learn that listening is indeed a skill, that most of us don't have it, and that to become a good listener requires hard work and discipline! I hope I have now improved, but it is not something I take for granted nowadays.

Spiritual friendship opens up the possibility of true dialogue—not just of conversation, but the sharing of our innermost being. This in itself is healing and liberating. When we lend a listening ear we are providing the opportunity for people to get in touch with their longings and desires, their hopes and their dreams, their fears and insecurities. As we listen to them we are also listening to God, for what we are seeking is to hear and recognize the voice of God in the midst of our ordinary lives. We invite people to talk and share, and together we work to explore, discover and discern what is going on in their lives at any given moment.

To listen attentively or actively requires real concentration, and to be truly present to another demands that we be absent from ourselves for a period in order to focus on the other. As we listen we may want to ask an occasional question for clarity, or to help the speaker focus their thinking. We listen for the pattern in what is being shared, seeking to find the deeper meaning in the words. We learn to read between the lines, noticing not only what is said but, often more importantly, what is not said. We notice, too, what the person's body language may be saying, too—a slight nervousness, a look of pain, a sense of shame or guilt. All the time we are listening to God and asking the Holy Spirit to give us wisdom and insight. We look for his nudges and promptings and listen for his words of revelation. We pray for the person who shares, too, in the pauses, asking God to guide them and to be with them as they talk.

Spiritual friends (mentors) offer wise counsel

It is important to remember that our role is not to 'fix' situations or to come up with solutions for people's problems. This is a great relief, and it means we can be relaxed in our role. Indeed, the best thing we can sometimes do is nothing—simply be there for the other person and by our very presence communicate God's affirming love. We can also expect to make a response to what is shared, however, and at the right time we can bring our own thoughts into the dialogue. Sometimes this may mean offering a few suggestions or alternatives for the person to think over. This can be helpful because they may not always be able to see the broader picture when they are locked into a situation. Often, in my own experience, it may mean confirming what the person has already been thinking. This kind of external confirmation can be so important in matters of guidance, for example. Occasionally, we may feel it right gently to challenge a person's thinking when they appear to have it wrong in some respect. We all have inadequate ideas about God, for instance, and sometimes wrong thinking in this area can lead to serious distortions in Christian living. I was so grateful to my spiritual mentor who on one occasion said to me, 'Tony, do you think what you've just said is actually true?' It shook me a little, but it made me rethink an inaccurate and damaging concept of God I had held for many years.

There may well be times when we will need to minister forgiveness to those who become aware either of their sin or of their sinfulness. This is often part of what God is doing in our lives as he prepares us for greater blessing. The privilege of affirming God's forgiveness is an authority that the Holy Spirit gives to us (John 20:21–23), and sometimes we need to hear the words of pardon in a voice we recognize if we are to be truly liberated. From time to time we will feel a prompting to pray specifically for the person, maybe with the laying on of hands, as they respond to what God the Spirit is doing in their lives. Throughout the process we are seeking to follow what God is doing, to allow the Spirit to be the director. We will never want to control or manipulate, to bully or cajole. We will always respect the person's freedom of conscience and their ability to hear God for themselves. We will never demand a response, only invite it.

Spiritual friends give continuing support

Some of my major life decisions have been made in the context of a mentoring relationship. As mentors we will also have the privilege of seeing people open up their lives to God in full and glad surrender. Remember that one of the goals of mentoring is to help individuals discover the will of God for their lives and then respond in obedience. We want to help people find their unique place in God's plan and purpose. When this kind of response is made—or any other kind for that matter—it is important that we show our willingness to continue to be there for them. It goes without saying that one of the best ways of showing our ongoing support is by our commitment to pray for the person on a regular basis. We can also keep in touch with them by phone, letter or email and be available outside formal mentoring times.

All mentoring relationships need 'boundaries'. One of these is to determine not only when a relationship begins but also for how long it will last. This is not necessarily a negative thing, for we need different mentors for different parts of the journey. Knowing that a mentoring relationship is secure for an agreed period actually gives strength and stability to it, especially when it comes to working through issues that will need more time, or when big decisions are about to be made.

Here follows a description of what might happen in a mentoring context: there is time to meet as friends and then the opportunity to share personally and meaningfully what is on our heart. Next comes the period of listening and discerning what God is saying, before finally we come to the phase where we draw things together and respond to what we feel God has said. As a mentor you will develop your style and unique ways of working, and because every mentoree is different, the process will never look the same twice anyway.

─────── *Chapter Five*───────

Reliable guides:
Qualities, skills and tools of a mentor

I was converted as a teenager in a small Methodist chapel in a Yorkshire mining village. I was not from a Christian family but had been brought up to go to Sunday school, attended a Church of England primary school and always had an awareness of God in my own heart. At the age of 14, I heard the gospel for the first time from a group of visiting Bible college students. With tears rolling down my cheeks I responded to their invitation to receive Christ as my Saviour. It was a deep and life-changing encounter. There was a real danger that the excitement might have worn off after the students had gone home, and I could have fallen by the wayside, spiritually speaking. Fortunately, several people came into my life at the right moment to help me on my way. None of these people (whose names have been changed in the following accounts) mentored me in a formal sense, but because they took me under their wings I was able to get established as a believer and begin to grow spiritually.

Bob was the first. He was the leader of the church youth group I attended, and soon after my conversion he invited me to join him for the summer months working at a Christian holiday centre. It was just about my first time away from home, and six weeks was a long time, but I loved every minute of it. Bob gave me my first taste of responsibility and of leadership as together we arranged outings and activities for the guests and led devotions. It was my first taste of public speaking, too, but Bob was always there to give encouragement and advice. Most of all, we had such fun together as we shared a room, and we would often be rolling about the floor laughing at something ridiculous that had been said or done. I learned from Bob that Christianity was enjoyable, adventurous and challenging. At the end of our second such summer I knew that God was calling me into full-time ministry.

Brian came along at about the same time, a teacher in the school I attended, with a strong Christian faith and a love of the outdoors. He took us away on many camping holidays and also held Bible studies in his home on Saturday evenings. About 20 of us would pack into his living room and enjoy an hour or so of Bible teaching. There was lots of fun and sometimes boisterous behaviour (I remember we broke the arm of his new settee!), but undergirding it all was a clear explanation of the gospel and what it meant to be a disciple. I guess I derived my love for the scriptures from Brian and learned the importance of Bible teaching and strong commitment to Jesus from him as well. When I decided to go to Bible college, it seemed natural to go to the same college where he had trained, and when it came to doing some preliminary study in Greek, of course it was Brian who helped me.

Alongside these two men there was also Phil, who took a group of young people (what we called the 'mission band') around the chapels in the area to preach and lead worship. We would each take a turn in some part of the service and, under Phil's watchful eye, practise carefully in private before going out and doing it for real. He would give us feedback and encourage us to use our gifts. I guess it was Phil who got me started in preaching, and I will always be grateful for the opportunities he gave me. I still have some of my notes from those days, and I'm embarrassed by the things I apparently said, but it didn't seem to put Phil off!

Later on Mike had a profound impact on my life. He had a prophetic ministry and taught us about life in the Spirit, and it was revolutionary. He was also strong on Bible meditation and prayer, and I guess it is from him I learned more about the inner life and the importance of our walk with God. He would often ask direct questions like, 'And what has God said to you today, Tony?' which kept me on my toes. When my wife and I worked overseas, I kept in touch with Mike and would often write to him for advice (if only there had been emails then!) When I was in church leadership in the UK it seemed natural to look to him for oversight. He stood by us through some tricky situations, often at personal cost, and was always available to us.

Most recently I have been helped in a more formal sense by Anne, a woman with a deep awareness of God and keen spiritual insight. Anne ran a retreat centre, and during the period in my own life when I was discovering contemplative spirituality, it was she who schooled me in this particular spiritual stream. I spent many wonderful days at her home, spending time with God, but also sharing my heart with Anne, and letting her wisdom speak into my life. Gentle but firm, she guided me through some of my own personal issues and helped me with some of my most significant decision-making. I would not be writing this today if it had not been for her willingness to spend so much time with me.

I could go on describing people who have been a help to me, and those who still are. My reason for sharing these stories, though, is that you may be able to identify some of the qualities and skills that are necessary in spiritual mentoring (whether formally or informally). It may be helpful at this point, before you read any further, to stop and think about the people who have helped you on your journey. Think about each one, and what they contributed to your life. Give thanks to God for them. Ask yourself, 'What qualities and skills did they have? Why was I so drawn to them, and how did they help me?'

Keith Anderson and Randy Reese talk about the power of 'spiritual attraction' in the mentoring process in their book *Spiritual Mentoring*,[1] by which they mean that we are usually drawn to mentors whom we admire and respect and who we feel (almost by intuition) can help us on our own journey. We see in them something that we would like to have in our own lives. As I share my own suggestions about the qualities, skills and tools needed for spiritual mentoring, remember that this reflects my own perspective. You can add (or subtract) from these suggestions as you wish.

It may also be helpful to say that I believe spiritual mentoring is a matter of gifting and calling. It is something that God places within us, for which the Holy Spirit uniquely gifts us and for which Christ prepares us during the whole of our lives. I don't think that we can train someone to be a spiritual mentor unless they first have this gifting and calling. Training will enrich and enhance a basic disposition, but training alone cannot produce spiritual mentors.

Qualities

Personal experience of Christ

Since we are talking about spiritual mentoring, it goes without saying that a mentor should be a spiritual person, and someone who knows Christ in a deep and intimate way. I think a mentor, almost by definition, is someone who is slightly ahead of the mentoree in the journey and should be at least a little more experienced in following Christ. Mentors should have a clear experience of conversion, have grown in grace, and still be passionately wanting to know more of Jesus (Philippians 3:7–10). As mentors we impart truth to others primarily by our personal example, and spiritual passion is more 'caught' than 'taught'.

Understanding of God's ways

If we are going to help others discern what God is doing in their lives, we should have some experience ourselves of discovering the will of God and discerning his work in our own lives. This means that mentors will almost certainly have 'lived a bit', since there is no substitute for experience. The kind of wisdom a mentor needs does not come from text books, seminars or classrooms but is born out of real-life situations. As we consistently follow Jesus over many years we begin to discern the patterns that mark God's ways, and we begin to recognize his handwriting, so to speak, in the events of daily life. In the words of the Psalmist: 'He made known his *ways* to Moses, his *deeds* to the people of Israel' (Psalm 103:7, italics mine).

In tune with the Holy Spirit

Since the Holy Spirit is the true spiritual mentor, it is important to develop a listening ear to be open to the promptings he may give as we listen to others. As we depend on the Spirit to guide us, he will help us make sense of what we are hearing, and prompt us with appropriate scriptures or helpful insights to share with the mentoree. More specifically, we can be open to receive words of wisdom and knowledge that may unlock problem areas (1 Corinthians 12:8). If we adopt a listening posture as a way of life, the Spirit will be able to drop into our minds significant thoughts at any time: 'The Sovereign Lord has given me an instructed tongue, to know the word that sustains the weary. He wakens me morning by morning, wakens my ear to listen like one being taught' (Isaiah 50:4).

Prayerfulness

The whole mentoring context is one of listening prayer, of course, for even as we listen to what is being shared we are holding the person up before God. Prayer beforehand not only expresses our own dependency upon God but can make it easier for people to share with us. Prayer following a mentoring situation can seal what has taken place and prevent Satan from undoing the good work that has taken place. It may be appropriate in the context of mentoring to offer the laying on of hands or prayer for ministry. Like the high priest of old, who had the names of the tribes of Israel inscribed upon his breastplate, those who mentor will have the names of the persons they guide written on their hearts.

Experience of suffering and failure

'Never trust a man who walks without a limp' is a saying that sums up this point. Someone who has known only success and achievement may not be the best person to help others since they are likely to believe that their way is the only right way, simply because it worked for them! They are more likely to be proud and arrogant than someone who has known failure and tasted defeat. The deepest lessons of the spiritual life are learned in the crucible, and those who have never been there themselves will not be reliable guides.

Out of his own experience of failure and recovery, the apostle Peter was changed from a pebble into a rock and became one who could reliably shepherd the flock of God. When he reminds us that 'your enemy the devil prowls around like a roaring lion looking for someone to devour' (1 Peter 5:8), we know that he speaks with the authority of experience. When he says, 'Resist him, standing firm in the faith' (v. 9), we know his advice is trustworthy since he has been there himself.

Availability

We cannot expect to mentor other people if we are out of reach all the time. Certainly mentoring operates best within certain boundaries and with clearly defined expectations, but the willingness to give quality time to those we mentor is essential. This may be in formal settings when times are agreed and appointments kept, or it may also happen more informally, for example in the context of relaxing, travelling together or working on the same project. This was surely how Jesus mentored his own disciples as they shared their lives together for those three important years. Time is one of our most precious resources, so making ourselves available to other people requires a degree of sacrifice.

Self-awareness and understanding of people

Knowing ourselves is one of the keys to personal growth and development. It is so easy to deceive ourselves, to live behind defensive walls and never to face up to our own shortcomings. Only those who know their own strengths and weaknesses and are prepared to be vulnerable will be able to mentor effectively since it requires us to be good students of humanity, especially our own.

Genuine love for people

We communicate the message that we accept those we mentor for who they are and as they are. Indeed what motivates us in mentoring is that we have a great love for people and want to see individuals reach their full potential. This doesn't mean that we are soft or turn a blind eye to shortcomings or sin. We can confront inappropriate behaviour when necessary and offer a challenge when it is needed but do so in a way that shows we value and believe in the individual. We have learned to speak the truth in love (Ephesians 4:15) and to love not with our own love but with the love of God.

Confidentiality

Mentoring relationships are built on the basis of trust and that means being able to hold a confidence. Generally speaking, people will open up to us only as they feel that they can trust us. They will usually try us out with a few minor confidences first, and only when they are sure that we will not break their trust will they share those things that are most important to them. It is a great privilege to be given another person's trust, and we must be sure to hold it with reverence and respect. If for any reason we feel we need the help and advice of a third party, we must ask permission before disclosing information to someone outside the mentoring relationship.

Encouragement

As mentors we must believe in those we are mentoring and operate on the basis of faith in the working of God in a person's life. This means we can remain optimistic and positive at all times, and can put strength into the mentorees. Someone has said that mentors speak three clear messages: it can be done; you're not alone; I believe in you. Like Barnabas, we operate with the spiritual gift of encouragement (Acts 4:36).

Skills

Skills differ from qualities in that they can be taught. These are learned behaviours that we can develop and improve.

Active listening

This is the ability truly to 'hear' what another person is saying (or sometimes not saying). Most of us assume that listening is easy, but usually our listening simply involves waiting for our turn to speak. We miss a lot of what the other person is saying simply because we are not listening.

I have already mentioned my own problems with listening. In order to improve, I had to learn how to focus consciously on what the other person was saying and to shut out my own thoughts. I had to learn to give them my full attention, not to interrupt them and to be comfortable with their silences. I had to learn how to reflect back to the person what I understood them to be saying, rather than assume I had taken it all in. This is why listening is hard work, and why after a time of truly listening to someone, you feel so tired! But truly listening to another person is one of the best gifts we can give them, and anyone who would take mentoring seriously should equip themselves by developing their skills as a listener.

Asking good questions

After listening skills, the ability to ask good questions is a high priority. In fact, as Bryn Hughes reminds us, 'The principal key to asking good questions is actually rooted in listening.'[2] We don't want to make a mentoring session feel like an inquisition, yet the use of good questions can encourage people to talk and to explore their deeper feelings. Jesus was always asking questions, of course, and we can learn from his example.

Open questions that require more than a simple 'yes' or 'no' answer are the best. These often begin with 'How?' or 'Why?' but must never sound threatening, so the tone of voice we use is important. Questions can help people describe a situation, identify their feelings and even explore the thinking that lies behind their emotions. Such exploration can be invaluable in identifying wrong belief systems and opening the way for the renewing of the mind.

Knowledge of the scriptures and the spiritual classics

Since we are talking here about *spiritual* mentoring and are doing so in the context of the Christian faith, a thorough knowledge of the Bible and the ability to relate it to the situation of our mentorees are valuable skills. It is in scripture that we discover the principles by which God works, and it is to the scriptures that we should point mentorees for their guidance and inspiration. Not only the teaching passages of scripture can be helpful but also the narrative sections, for God has written many of his most important lessons into the lives of his people.

In addition to scripture we can learn much wisdom from some

of the spiritual classics, which have enriched and informed God's people down the centuries. Of course it is difficult to itemize them all here, but some of the most important would include: *The Dark Night of the Soul* by St John of the Cross, *The Interior Castle* by Teresa of Avila and *The Practice of the Presence of God* by Brother Lawrence. Some of the great writers on the inner life are worth reading, too— Madam Guyon, Julian of Norwich, Andrew Murray, Henri Nouwen, Thomas Kelly, Thomas Merton, Evelyn Underhill, Watchman Nee, A.W. Tozer, to name just a few. And we must not forget that there are many contemporary writers who will enrich our lives and deepen our awareness of Christian spirituality—Richard Foster, Joyce Huggett, Dallas Willard, Eugene Peterson, Brennan Manning and Margaret Silf would be among my own favourites. By their wisdom and insight these great writers actually mentor us through their writings and increase our understanding and deepen our experience of the inner life.

Tools

Just has a mechanic will have a set of tools with which to work, so a mentor can gather together practical ways of helping people discover themselves and engage with God.

The Bible

As mentors we will be soaked in the word of God and will also be able to use scripture appropriately in the mentoring process. Jesus said, 'Every teacher of the law who has been instructed about the kingdom of heaven is like the owner of a house who brings out of his storeroom new treasures as well as old' (Matthew 13:52). The wise mentor will be looking to point the mentoree to relevant Bible passages to read and verses on which to meditate. We will know how to engage people with scripture through such means as imaginative reading or *Lectio Divina* (an ancient way of engaging with God by listening to scripture as it is read and then responding to what is given to us by the Holy Spirit—for a fuller description see Appendix B). It is helpful always to seek to connect what is happening in the mentoring process to the background of the scriptures.

Personality tests

There are many of these available and, wisely applied, they can be really helpful in developing self-awareness. One of these tools is the Enneagram, but my own favourite is the Myers-Briggs Personality Type Indicator ®. I find that it gives people a useful framework into which they can place all the information they already have about themselves. It helps them not only to appreciate themselves but also begin to understand what makes other people 'tick'. It has many relevant applications, especially regarding the impact of personality on the spiritual life. Of course you may not have the training to administer either of these 'tools', but an understanding of them will greatly enhance your ability to help others.

Spiritual exercises

These are a variety of simple, practical ways by which we can encourage others to engage with God. It was Ignatius Loyola in 16th-century Spain who led the way in this regard with his book *The Spiritual Exercises* and this remains perhaps the most widely used tool today, although it is often adapted for modern use. The three searching questions, 'Who am I? Where am I? How am I?' are taken from Ignatius, as is the commonly used practice of imaginative Bible reading (where we are asked to imagine ourselves inside a story and experience it from within). Margaret Silf has helped to popularize the Exercises in her book *Landmarks*,[3] which is a great resource for all spiritual mentors. More recently, Ray Simpson has produced a book of simple exercises called *The Joy of Spiritual Fitness*.[4] I include in Appendix A some of the exercises that I use myself as further examples. It is worth building up your own collection of exercises.

The great danger of providing lists of qualities, skills and tools is that at the end of them no one feels qualified! It is not my intention to discourage you but rather to encourage you to continue your own personal development as a mentor and grow into this most important role. Affirm yourself for the qualities that are already in place in your life (no false modesty, please!) and ask God to help you in areas in which you feel weak. Think about sharpening the skills you already have and how you may develop new ones.

Above all, commit yourself to God for this task, asking for his anointing to rest upon you, for this is spiritual ministry and it can only be done in the power of the Spirit.

⊹

——— *Chapter Six* ———

The scenic route:
Developing spiritual awareness

There are usually two ways to get to any particular place—the direct way or the scenic way. Most of us choose the quickest direction, opting for the motorways, so we can arrive at our destination as soon as possible. Few of us have time for the slower, more scenic way, and it means we miss the opportunity to enjoy the beautiful countryside around us. This is how we live, too. We become so busy reaching our goals in life, so obsessed with meeting our targets and deadlines, that we have no time to notice what is happening in our lives. We are so absorbed with the business of living that we fail to recognize the presence of God.

Perhaps the greatest contribution a spiritual mentor can make to another person's life is to help them awaken to the presence of God, to become aware of what God is doing in their life and then make a faith-filled response. Benner calls this 'soul attunement' and says that facilitating such awareness is the master goal of spiritual direction. This is how he puts it: 'God constantly reaches out, seeking our attention, seeking to be known. We walk through this world oblivious, failing to notice him. We are so wrapped up in ourselves—our plans, our worries, our activities—that we fail to see him. Anything that helps us develop a receptive posture of openness to the Divine prepares us to encounter the God who constantly reveals himself.'[1]

Spiritual mentoring will almost certainly involve a degree of tutoring in spiritual awareness. It is so easy for us to miss the presence of God, to fail to hear his voice. God appears to be often in the shadows, as it were, and often speaks in the 'gentle whisper' (1 Kings 19:12). We have to be attentive to his presence if we are to benefit fully from his nearness. God is all around us, and we live in a God-bathed world, but this does not mean we are always aware of him. In mentoring others we will need to concentrate on helping them discover the already present action of God. A large part of what we do will focus on simply enabling them to recognize what God is about.

Jacob is a good example of someone engrossed in the business of living. Having been sent by his father Isaac to find himself a wife among the daughters of Laban, he is (understandably) absorbed in his task. No doubt, too, his mind is filled with anxious thoughts about his brother Esau, whom he had cheated, and who was now seeking to kill him. When he stops for the night 'at a certain place' (Genesis 28:11), he has a dream in which God speaks to him. When he awakes he is suddenly and dramatically conscious of God. 'Surely the Lord is in this place, and I was not aware of it,' he says (v. 16). 'How awesome is this place! This is none other than the house of God; this is the gate of heaven' (v. 17). It is possible to be within an inch of God and yet not be alert to his presence.

Or think of the two disciples on the road to Emmaus. Disappointed and dejected, they are so preoccupied with their own negative thoughts that when the risen Jesus comes alongside them they fail to register that he is anything other than a fellow traveller. 'They were kept from recognizing him,' as Luke tells it (24:16). It requires a moment of special revelation for their eyes to be opened. 'When he was at table with them, he took bread, gave thanks, broke it and began to give it to them. Then their eyes were opened and they recognized him' (v. 31). And what about Mary Magdalene in the garden? She is overcome with grief and sadness and assumes that the risen Lord is merely the gardener. 'At this, she turned round and saw Jesus standing there, but she did not realize that it was Jesus' (John 20:14). Sorrow prevented her from recognizing him.

Only when he calls her by name does she awaken to his presence.

How, then, can we help people to become more spiritually aware?

God in the world around us

We can help them, firstly, to *notice God in the world around them*. Creation itself speaks to us loudly of God in a way that is clear and unmistakable, no matter where we are or what our own language is: 'The heavens declare the glory of God; the skies proclaim the work of his hands. Day after day they pour forth speech; night after night they display knowledge. There is no speech or language where their voice is not heard. Their voice goes out into all the earth, their words to the ends of the world' (Psalm 19:1–4). We can train ourselves really to take note of the world around us and let its grandeur and majesty speak to us of the greatness of God. When we wake to a beautiful sunrise, catch a glimpse of a cloud-filled sky or stand awestruck before a breathtaking panorama, we can stop and pause and savour the moment, allowing it to point us to God and helping us to connect with him at a deep inner level.

As well as speaking to us of the 'bigness' of God in these general terms, creation can also speak to us personally and individually, for God has filled the created order with his word. Again, if we are alive to it, we can hear God speak to us even as we encounter his creation. This is why Jesus trained his disciples to open their eyes and really look around them—at the birds flying overhead or at the flowers in the meadows nearby, for instance (Matthew 6:25–30). He knew that they would find there parables of nature that would teach them rich spiritual lessons about the Father's care over them and his provision for them, easing their anxious hearts. Once we realize that creation is alive with God and develop the discipline of looking closely at things, we shall not find it hard to become aware of the God who surrounds us and who calls to us constantly.

A simple exercise that has helped me to become more aware of God in the world around me, and which I continually recommend to others, is what is called an 'awareness walk'. In this we simply step outside—and go for a walk. We do so intentionally, with the prayer that God will guide our steps and with the desire that we will meet with him. Then, as we walk, we 'notice what we notice'. Anything that grabs our attention, catches our eye or to which we seem drawn becomes an occasion for thoughtful reflection. What does it say to me? How might God be speaking to me through this? What lessons could I learn from it? I have found that because I use this exercise quite often, my awareness has increased tremendously. I realize now how frequently the Spirit draws my attention to significant things around me, even when I am not consciously on an 'awareness walk'. It is as if my spiritual sensitivity has increased and with it my awareness of God.

God in our daily lives

Secondly, we can help people to *find God in their daily lives*. It is great to have mountain-top experiences when God's presence is amazingly real to us, but much of life is lived on the plain of the mundane, and we must be able to discover God's presence there as well. We must be able to find him in the routine of our domestic chores, in the challenges of family life, in the complexities of working environments, in the enjoyment of our leisure activities and pastimes. Rather than thinking that God is not interested in such down-to-earth matters, we should recognize that a God who became incarnate in Jesus and entered our world is interested and involved in all that happens to us.

A simple exercise that helps many people to see the footprints of God in the ordinariness of life is called the 'prayer of examen'. It involves thinking over the events of our day and replaying them in our minds rather like a video recording. With the help of the Spirit we ask some simple questions that will help us identify the presence of God in all that has happened to us. Who did I meet today? Did anyone reveal something of God's love to me in their kindness or compassion? Was I in some small way able to reveal God's love to someone else? What am I thankful for today? Is there anything I feel sorry about? Did anything happen to challenge my faith? Was I aware of God speaking to me at all? Such a review of the day is not meant to show us where we have failed but where we have succeeded. We are not to judge ourselves for times when we 'missed it' but rather give thanks for the growth we can see in ourselves. Again, with constant practice this simple discipline will become a means by which we can enhance our awareness of God's presence day by day.

Alongside this we can encourage others with what Jean-Pierre de Caussade called the 'sacrament of the present moment'. This 18th-century French spiritual director encouraged individuals not to become too dependent upon spiritual guides but to find God for themselves in the ups and downs of normal life. 'To discover God in the smallest and most ordinary things, as well as in the greatest, is to possess a rare and sublime faith,'[2] is how he put it. This will mean living in line with the recognition that 'this is the day that the Lord has made; let us rejoice and be glad in it' (Psalm 118:24). In other words, this moment is the most important moment I have, because it is the only moment I have. Therefore I should experience it to the full and be alive to God in the here and now.

Too many people live their lives locked into their regrets of the past or awaiting their dreams for the future, while missing God in the present moment that envelops them. We make a sacrament of the present by recognizing that the God who gave us the day will be in the day with us. He is there in our waking, our eating, our working and our sleeping, a constant companion and guide. As John Ortberg says, 'This moment is God's irreplaceable gift to you. Most of all, this is the moment that matters because this is the moment where God is. If you are going to be with God at all, you must be with him *now*—in this moment... In the same way that every lungful of air gives life to our body, every moment in time can—if we learn to let it—give life to our soul. *This moment* is as God-filled as any we have ever lived.'³

God at work in circumstances

There is a third way by which we can help others to develop their awareness of God. We can encourage them to *see God at work in their circumstances*. Normally we have no problems in recognizing the activity of God in the positive aspects of life. Although there is always a temptation to take things for granted, it is relatively easy to develop an attitude of thankfulness and to acknowledge the goodness of God in all that daily brings joy and gladness to us. It is perhaps a little harder to see the gracious hand of God in our lives when a situation is not going so well, yet scripture clearly teaches us that God is at work in all things. As Paul confidently asserted: 'We know that in all things God works for the good of those who love him, who have been called according to his purpose' (Romans 8:28).

A man once met with his spiritual mentor at a time when things had gone badly for him, and he was angry with God. His life seemed to be in pieces, and he accusingly blurted out his question, 'Where is God when I need him most?' The wise mentor affirmed that his question was a good one and, changing the tone of the question to one of enquiry, replied, 'Yes, indeed, where is God at this time of your need?' He said that if the man were willing to offer the question as a prayer, he (the mentor) would join him in seeking together to discover God's presence even in the darkness. Slowly the man's anger subsided, and he agreed to pray for eyes to see God in his circumstances.

Over the next few days he continued to feel pain and to question God but he also continued to pray that he might find God in his circumstances. One morning a portion of scripture leapt off the page as he read: 'For darkness is as light to you' (Psalm 139:12). 'I realized,' he said afterwards, 'that God has no problem seeing me in the dark; it's just that I have a problem seeing him.' Certainly it is often with hindsight that we can best determine how God has shaped and formed us during the hard times and appreciate the many lessons God teaches us during such periods. It is not the job of the mentor to try to 'fix' things or to come up with clever answers to difficult questions. We are called simply to walk with people through the valleys of life and to be there for them as they 'trace the rainbow through the rain'.[4]

God in other people

The fourth way of increasing the awareness of God is by helping people *to recognize God in the people they meet.* God has many ways of coming to us, and often his presence will be hidden in the form of people all around us. Jesus highlighted this in the parable of the sheep and goats (Matthew 25:31–46). Here Jesus identifies himself with those who are hungry, thirsty, homeless, naked, sick or in prison. When we help them, we are in fact helping him; when we reject them, we reject him. This was the simple philosophy behind the amazing work of Mother Teresa in the slums of Calcutta. It is a way of looking at people which recognizes them as made in the image of God, created to know and love him. Certainly that image has been marred, but enough remains in each individual to mean that we must treat them with dignity and respect.

In the course of an ordinary day we will meet many people. I know for myself that it is easy to pass them by without really noticing them, or bothering to spend time with them. People easily become part of the landscape of our lives, the 'extras' in the film of which we are the star. They become little more than machines, valued for their usefulness. So the girl at the supermarket checkout desk, the clerk in the booking office, the man who brings the mail—each of them can become absorbed into the background of our lives, nameless faces without meaning or significance. Alternatively, we can ask for the grace to see people as Jesus saw them and to see Jesus in them. We can treat them as people who carry the image of God, as people who have stories to tell, who are worthy of our attention. Then, as we reach out to them with the love of God, we shall find that we are actually meeting Christ himself. As we relate to them we are relating to him.

It has been said that spiritual growth is simply increasing our capacity to experience the presence of God. As we journey alongside others on the spiritual journey, it will be our privilege to help them to enjoy the scenery along the way by becoming more attentive to God. We will want to help them to tune their ears to the sound of God's voice, to open their eyes to his presence and to recognize his activity in every part of their lives. As together we learn to do this more and more, we will become less absorbed with ourselves and more occupied with God.

❖

—————— *Chapter Seven* ——————

A sense of direction:
The gift of discernment

If developing spiritual awareness is the master goal of direction, then the gift of discernment is the greatest asset a mentor can bring to the process. We can liken it to that intuitive sense of direction which some people have that helps them to find their way. It is more a matter of instinct than knowledge. The gift of discernment likewise serves as a compass for spiritual travellers. It helps them to navigate their way through a multiplicity of choices and options. It enables them to recognize and choose the right path when they might otherwise be confused.

The Latin root of the word 'discern' (*discernere*) means to separate or distinguish, while the Greek root (*diakrisis*) means to test or distinguish good and evil. One definition suggests that discernment is the process whereby we find that which is authentic and valuable (like panning for gold or biting a coin to see if it is real). Another says it is the possession of immediate and direct insight. Each of these explanations gives helpful clues as to what we mean by discernment. The definition that comes closest to summing it up for me suggests that discernment is seeing the heart of the matter with spiritual eyes; seeing God's viewpoint; seeing beyond the surface of events, beyond the immediate and transient.

Discernment is vital in the life of the church. We are called upon to 'test the spirits' (1 John 4:1), because Satan continually seeks to hinder the work of God by sending false prophets and false teaching. The New Testament is full of the confusion caused by unscrupulous people and wayward teachings. Church leaders are also called to distinguish what is of God and what is not; which words come from God, and which may arise from self or human imagination. They are to 'weigh' prophecies and inspirational messages given in church, for instance, on the basis that anything which is of the Spirit will glorify Jesus (1 Corinthians 12:1–3). When it comes to spiritual guidance, discernment is equally vital. Discernment is primarily a gift from God, although we can develop the ability to discern, and there are steps in the process of discernment which anyone can follow. Paul includes it among the gifts of the Spirit, describing it as 'distinguishing between spirits' (1 Corinthians 12:10). Many charismatic Christians interpret this in a very narrow sense, seeing it as the ability to recognize the presence and activity of demonic forces, but most commentators see a much wider application than this. It is usually described as the ability to recognize the true source of spiritual activity, whether from God, the devil or merely human origin.

Discernment in the broader sense comes as a positive inner feeling that something is the right thing to do, or equally a strong interior sense of unease, suggesting something may in fact be wrong. Paul experienced this as he considered where to go during his second missionary journey (Acts 16:6–10). He would have pressed on into Asia, but 'having been kept by the Holy Spirit from preaching the word [there]' (v. 6), he turned his attention to Bithynia. However, 'the Spirit of Jesus would not allow them to' (v. 7), so they waited. Then came the vision of the man from Macedonia and the conclusion that this was indeed where God wanted them to go.

Since discernment is primarily a gift from God, we should not be surprised to see that it is normally given to us in the context of prayer. It is our humble dependency upon God that moves us to seek for his wisdom. Perhaps the best example of this is Solomon's prayer as he became king. He could have asked for anything, but he chose wisdom. 'So give your servant a discerning heart to govern

your people and to distinguish between right and wrong,' he prayed
(1 Kings 3:9). Most of us know only too well our lack of wisdom
and that is why we, too, are invited to ask God to impart his wisdom
to us. 'If any of you lacks wisdom he should ask God,' says James,
'who gives generously to all without finding fault, and it will be
given him' (James 1:5). Good mentors operate out of a 'leaning on
God' mentality and soak their conversations in a prayerful seeking
for God's direction.

There is also a wisdom that comes from the benefit of 'lived
experience', and mentors can call on this as they listen to the stories
of others. This is one of the reasons why spiritual mentoring fits
better into the second half of life. It is not that we want to force our
experience upon others, or to say that what happened for us must
be the norm for everyone else; however, having observed God at
work in our own lives and in the lives of others over a sustained
period of time, we will be more equipped to recognize the common
threads and patterns in the activity of God. A doctor diagnosing his
patients' symptoms will instinctively call on past experience to
guide him, and a 'physician of souls' will wisely do the same. 'In the
shared work of mentoring,' say Anderson and Reese, 'we learn how
to see connections, how to recognize plot and how to enjoy the
unfolding story line of our own lives and the lives of others, but it
takes the discipline of noticing, the practice of attention, to make
those connections.'[1]

It is worth saying, too, that discernment comes most easily when
we are surrendered fully to God and open to doing his will,
whatever that may be. We will find discernment difficult if we have
predetermined ideas of what God should do, or if we set conditions
about what we will or will not do. Only when we have offered
ourselves fully to God, and when our minds are being renewed, will
we be able to 'test and approve what God's will is' (Romans 12:2).
Mentors, knowing this truth for themselves, will gently help their
mentorees come to this place of readiness for discernment. They do
not seek to do the work of discernment on behalf of others but

rather to facilitate a process of co-discernment. They use their gift of discernment to ask the right questions, explore the most important issues and to signal when things are moving in the right direction. Their prayer is the same as that of Paul for the church at Philippi: 'And this is my prayer; that your love may abound more and more in knowledge and depth of insight, so that you may be able to discern what is best...' (Philippians 1:9–10). They do not seek to keep mentorees in a relationship of dependency but rather to liberate them into the maturity of hearing God for themselves.

Stephen Bryant has said:

Spiritual discernment makes operational our faith that an ever present Guide... is present to lead us in the way of truth and love as individuals and congregations. It opens our sails as a church to the Spirit whose winds we believe are always blowing and will move us closer to Christ, closer to one another, and closer to the world that God wills.[2]

Through the process of discernment we are seeking to be led into the right path, the way of truth and love. We need discernment to understand our own hearts, to interpret what God may be doing in our lives and decide the best course of action at moments of transition. By carefully listening, asking appropriate questions, and suggesting possibilities, spiritual mentors seek, with the help of the Spirit, to guide their mentorees in the right direction.

When it comes to discerning the right path in moral choices a popular move is to ask the simple question, 'What would Jesus do?' Here we bring our understanding of the life and teaching of Jesus to bear on our own ethical questions and imagine how he might respond, choosing to do only that which we feel would be in line with his own example. Another common principle is to see how a proposed action aligns with what we understand to be the teaching of scripture. 'What does scripture say?' is another key question. Again, we would not wish to act in any way contrary to what the Bible teaches, and so this principle becomes a way of discernment for us.

Other issues are less clear and may well involve the weighing up of two or more permissible directions. Jeanette Bakke, an experienced spiritual director from the US, has helpfully outlined an approach to discernment that she uses. While recognizing that discernment is not necessarily an ordered affair, there are common elements in the process:[3]

- Intentionally inviting the Spirit to speak to us, while asking for grace to recognize his intentions and interpret them accurately.
- Deciding what the focus of the discernment process is—what are we seeking?
- Using scripture, prayer and other means of gathering and evaluating information.
- Continuing to pray throughout the discernment process.
- Arriving at a provisional resolution.
- Testing the resolution.
- Moving forward on the basis of the decision and noticing what transpires.

Associated with the process of discernment is the belief that when we recognize and choose God's leading, our hearts will become peaceful, settled and quiet. This is often based on Colossians 3:15, which speaks of the peace of God acting as 'umpire' in such situations. It is, of course, possible to deceive ourselves and to be 'at peace' about a wrong course of action, especially if it is one we are determined to pursue anyway. This is where an objective presence of a mentor can save us from self-deception. Generally speaking we can assume that, if we are truly open to doing God's will, whatever that may be, we will experience a deep inner harmony between our thoughts and our feelings when we have made the right choice. This is the kind of alignment (or interior stability, as it has been called) that Paul speaks about following the deliberation of the Council of Jerusalem in Acts 15: 'It seemed good to the Holy Spirit and to us' (v. 28). Even if the decision is a costly one, there will be peace, and even if we encounter difficulties along the way, the inner assurance will remain.

We cannot talk of discernment and the process of discerning without mentioning (again) the Spiritual Exercises of Ignatius of Loyola. Born into a wealthy Spanish family in 1491, Ignatius became a soldier but was injured in battle. During his convalescence he was converted to Christ through meditating on his own experiences, and through reading the only book available to him at the time, which was a book about the life of Jesus. He quickly grew in his faith and was gifted in leading others into a deeper experience of God. He was a catalyst for renewal within the Roman Catholic Church and wrote down his notes from helping others in the form of his now famous Spiritual Exercises as a guide for other spiritual directors. They were originally intended to be used in a retreat setting over 30 days, but the principles they contain have been widely adapted to fit other contexts. They have without doubt been the most formative influence upon the development of the ministry of spiritual direction, and Ignatian spirituality has profoundly shaped the modern retreat movement.

The Exercises themselves divide into four weeks of sessions designed to be worked through with the help of a spiritual guide. The first week involves self-examination, clearing the debris from our lives and preparing ourselves to listen, and looks at motives and desires. The second week concentrates on the Gospel story and, through an imaginative entering into the narratives, seeks to turn the focus towards Christ and Christ-likeness. The third week concentrates on the passion of Christ, inviting us to appreciate all that he has done for us but also to connect our sufferings with his and thus to deepen our discipleship. The final week celebrates the resurrection of Christ and encourages a growing intimacy with God as attention is given to the love of God.

These four stages have become a paradigm which many spiritual mentors use, especially in the retreat setting. If we follow the stages, we begin with taking a long, hard look at ourselves, before turning our attention to Jesus; then we focus attention on our becoming like Christ and in preparing ourselves for his service. Throughout there is an emphasis on various styles of prayer, the importance of personal reflection, different ways of engaging with scripture and practical ways by which we can discern the working of God in our lives. The total impact of the programme has been summed up like this: 'intimate knowledge of Christ, that I might be *with* him, become *like* him and live *for* him.'[4]

Ignatius helps us most of all in discerning the movements within our own hearts, and he includes in the Exercises some practical rules that help us to recognize what is taking place within us. While many evangelical teachers would urge us to depend on facts rather than feelings, Ignatius encourages us to embrace our feelings and notice what is happening in our souls as a way of becoming more aware what God is actually doing. For him, the discernment of spirits is about noticing which spirit is influencing our feelings and behaviour, so that by distinguishing them we can receive the good and reject the bad. By 'spirits' he is talking about those affective stirrings of the heart (such as joy, sadness, hope, fear, peace, anxiety and so on) together with their related thoughts, which both influence our life of faith and progress towards God.

Ignatius identifies the stirrings of the soul with two basic descriptions: 'consolation' and 'desolation'. He uses these words in a particular sense. Consolation (from a Latin root meaning 'towards the sun') refers to the movement towards God which strengthens faith and love and our desire to do God's will. Desolation, however (from the Latin signifying 'away from the sun'), describes the movement which draws us away from God, weakening faith and love and the desire to do God's will. Ignatius sets his rules of discernment in the first week of the exercises, for this is the period of self-awareness, when we need to discern clearly whether the direction of our heart is towards God or not.

Consolation, then, is the interior movement of the soul when we feel full of love for God. It is a movement within us created by the

Holy Spirit, who sheds the love of God abroad in our hearts (Romans 5:5). It is the kind of experience that the two disciples had on the road to Emmaus when their hearts burned within them (Luke 24:32). It is the Holy Spirit bearing witness with our spirit that we are the children of God (Romans 8:16), bringing us an inner assurance and confidence. Such moments of consolation can occur when things are going well for us but also when we are facing difficulty and trial. God comes near to remind us that he is with us. We should not be afraid of such movements with us, for they are often the confirmation we need that we are doing God's will, and they can inspire us to acts of faith and devotion.

Desolation, by contrast, describes the condition of the soul when we feel apathy and a sense of coldness towards God. Outwardly all may be well, but inwardly we may find we have little desire for prayer or worship, and instead our hearts are drawn after the things of the world. We may feel a sense of separateness from God, a darkness of soul when we feel despair and want to give up. Like the Psalmist we cry out, 'Why are you downcast, O my soul? Why so disturbed within me?' (Psalm 42:5). While such moments may have natural causes (illness or tiredness, for example), sometimes God allows such times to correct us, to test our faith and help us grow in humility.

Ignatius gives some clear guidelines to help us navigate our way through such periods of desolation. Firstly, do not change course at such a moment, and refuse to reverse any decision you made in prayer before this. In other words, do not doubt in the darkness what God told you in the light. Secondly, persevere in prayer, worship and service no matter how low you feel. In fact, do the very opposite of what you 'feel' like doing. So the time when you least want to pray is in fact the best time to pray, even if it is difficult. Thirdly, remember that desolation is always temporary. Expect the clouds to lift and the sun to shine again.

It will be clear how important it is to help individuals discern what is taking place within them. We need to help them discern which mood is operational within them, and what direction this is taking them—whether towards God or away from God. Having recognized this, we can then act accordingly to go with the flow of God's Spirit or resist the pull of self and Satan. Thus there are three stages in this process of discernment: be aware of what is happening within you; understand the source of the movement; take action either to accept or reject this movement.

It has to be said that no human process can ever protect us from mistakes or failure or guarantee us absolute certainty. Often we will need to live with uncertainty, ambiguity and mystery. However, the practice of discernment can become a way of life, and this is what we hope will develop in the lives of those whom we mentor. We trust that as we journey together they will develop their own sense of direction.

⁌

—————— *Chapter Eight* ——————

Road maps and guidebooks: Insights for busy mentors

I love maps. Whenever I go to a new place, say on holiday, the first thing I do is to buy a map of the local area and try to get my bearings. Even in these days of satellite navigation, when I drive I still use my trusty road atlas. I enjoy the challenge of working out a route for myself, rather than being told by a disembodied voice where I should turn left or right!

On the spiritual journey it is helpful for us to have some idea of where we are and what might lie ahead. Of course the Bible gives us a sense of direction but it doesn't map out the way in a systematic sense. The Holy Spirit applies scripture to our lives as we go along. Jesus is the way (John 14:6) and, as long as we fix our eyes on him and follow his promptings, we shall not get lost. However, when we are trying to help others on the journey and share in their spiritual formation, it is useful to have an overview in our mind of what we might call a normal Christian growth pattern. We hold such 'road maps' lightly, of course, because we are aware that no two journeys are exactly the same, and we would not want to impose our own experience on to others or squeeze them into a predetermined mould. Nevertheless, an idea of where the journey might take us is bound to be helpful. In this chapter I want to share some of the 'maps and guidebooks' to the Christian pathway that I have found most useful.

The evangelical tradition to which I belong has normally pictured the Christian life in three clear stages—justification (being made right with God), sanctification (the process of becoming like Christ) and glorification (all that awaits us in heaven). In practice, and as far as spirituality is concerned, this is often reduced to two phases— coming to faith and being converted, followed by discipleship and a life of service. The emphasis soon becomes very much focused on doing things for God, and often little attention is given to the inner life. Admittedly, there is now a growing interest in spiritual formation, but generally evangelicals have been weak on spirituality. This explains why some contemporary evangelicals feel they have reached a plateau in their own spiritual growth within their own tradition and need to look outside its boundaries if further growth is to be maintained.

Roman Catholic spirituality, by contrast, has given much attention to the inner life journey, and this is reflected in many of the spiritual classics. A fourfold process of growth is generally acknowledged:[1]

- **Awakening:** This is the first movement of God in the soul and represents our becoming aware of God's presence and our own sinfulness. This is both a comfort and a threat and leaves us with a choice of whether or not we will respond. For some there is quite a struggle before they eventually decide to walk through the door that has opened before them into a whole new way of being.
- **Purgation:** This represents the stage of bringing our behaviour, attitudes and desires in line with the will of God. Initially this will mean repenting of the obvious sins in our lives and making a clean break with the past. Later it will deal with matters that are not necessarily wrong but are unhelpful for our further progress. More growth takes place as we deal with 'blind spots' in our lives, the unconscious sins and omissions which the Spirit reveals to us. Finally we are able to examine our heart motivations and inner attitudes in order to bring these, too, in line with God's will for us.
- **Illumination:** At this stage we give ourselves over to God completely, allowing him to be Lord of our lives and surrendering our

will to his. We learn to trust God for the whole of life and discover more of his presence within us. Prayer now becomes
communion, and the Holy Spirit is able to form the fruit of
the Spirit in our lives in great abundance. Liberated from self-
centredness, our lives are able to impact on others through
selfless service and loving ministry.

- **Union:** We now begin to enjoy the blessing of a complete oneness
with God, an abandonment to him that is akin to the best of
marriages—the two have become one. This stage may involve
times of deep spiritual ecstasy, but also moments of seeming
abandonment: what is called the dark night of the senses, or that
even deeper experience, the dark night of the soul—when we are
left with God alone in order to discover that he is all we need or
desire.

The terms used in this description of the classical Christian
pilgrimage will be new to some, but I think the stages of growth are
easily recognized, apart from perhaps the last one, the stage of
union. This is partly because few people reach this stage, and when
they do they tend to be labelled as 'mystics' and are not well understood by others. The contemporary purpose-driven church has little
time for those it considers 'other-worldly', and life itself does not
provide much opportunity for the kind of time and space needed to
develop such interiority.

Further, there is a real danger here of striving after a union with
God which, according to scripture, we already have. We have been
made one with him by grace and joined to him as a branch is joined
to the vine (John 15:5). I think this is one of the main differences
between evangelical and Roman Catholic approaches to spirituality.
Evangelicals would emphasize much more the truth that 'by grace
I already am' rather than strive to be something that we are not
yet. We certainly will need to grow into our identity as those who
are already 'in Christ' (2 Corinthians 5:17), but we don't need to get
there by ourselves or by our own efforts. The fact that God has

placed me 'in Christ' (1 Corinthians 1:30) is incentive enough to make oneness with him a reality in my daily life. What it does remind us of, though, is the fact that there is still plenty more to aim for when it comes to knowing God. None of us can say we have arrived. There is always more to discover and explore.

Dr Bobby Clinton, a professor at Fuller Theological Seminary in California, has developed another 'road map', which I have personally found very helpful. It is based on his reading and study of both scripture and Christian biographies and is particularly appropriate when working with leaders.[2] He identifies six stages in leadership development:

- **Sovereign foundations:** God works providentially in our circumstance and life experience not only to bring us to himself but also to build into our lives character traits that will later be used in ministry.
- **Inner-life growth:** Either through informal mentoring or more formal training the leader prepares for ministry, but other key lessons are being learned about prayer and hearing God, facing trials and being obedient to God's will. Character is further developed and there will be some form of ministry involvement.
- **Ministry maturing:** The leader now begins to identify and use his or her spiritual gifts, and starts to learn something of the complexities of interpersonal relationships within the body of Christ. God is working primarily *in* the leader, not *through* the leader, being concerned about potential, not productivity. This can be frustrating for emerging leaders who want to see things happen.
- **Life maturing:** Now, having identified gifting, the leader begins to work effectively and fruitfully, discovering that 'ministry flows out of being'. There may be times of isolation, crisis and conflict. Communion with God becomes more important at this stage.
- **Convergence:** God moves the leader into a role in which who they are and what they do coincide, so they reach maximum

fruitfulness. Gifts, experience and ministry come together in a satisfying mix. Not all reach this stage, and guidance needs to focus on helping the leader find a role which enables them to have maximum effectiveness.

- **Afterglow or celebration:** After a lifetime of ministry comes recognition and influence on a broad level and with younger leaders. Time is spent guiding others.

While Clinton's model is designed primarily with leadership development in mind, again we can see and recognize phases of growth that are common to all. Leaders particularly need to receive spiritual mentoring, and they will be drawn to it especially in the transition points of their ministries. Clinton helpfully identifies what he calls 'process items': the activities, people and problems that God allows to come into our lives as he shapes and develops us. The wise mentor will look out for these when listening to anyone in a leadership role.

The model which I have found most helpful, and which I think most accurately describes my own experience (and therefore my approach to mentoring) is that proposed by Janet Hagberg and Robert Guelich in *The Critical Journey*.[3] Their attempt to identify some of the milestones on the journey of faith suggests six key stages:

- **Recognition of God:** At this stage we first become aware of God, be it through a natural awareness of his existence that has always been with us, or through a sense of awe as we encounter him in the world he made, or through a sense of need for forgiveness or help with the problems of life. Faith is childlike and enthusiastic.
- **The life of discipleship:** Now we get involved with a group of other believers and begin to learn more about God. We learn what we have to do to become part of the group and happily follow a leader we respect. We begin to identify our gifts and special contribution and may seek responsibility. Faith is secure

and we carry a sense of rightness about what we believe. We are happy to be a good follower.

- **The productive life:** Faith is now expressed by working for God and, having found our unique place in the faith community, we take on more responsibility, even coming into a leadership position. The emphasis is on productivity and success. Roles, titles and recognition may be important. This may be time when we take on further training and make decisions about 'full-time' ministry.

- **The journey inward:** Here faith is rediscovering God. This may come about through a crisis of faith and be accompanied by a loss of certainty. There may well be a search for a new direction and not necessarily for answers. Having lived so much in the outer world, we now give our attention to the inner world. God is released from the 'box' of our own understanding and tradition.

- **The wall:** Although strictly part of stage 4 (the journey inward), this experience is deemed so critical that it is treated separately. 'The wall' represents our will meeting God's will face to face. We decide anew whether we are willing to surrender and let God direct our lives.[4] It is a pivotal moment in the journey but often a place of mystery, and it is different for everyone. All our defences and false identities are exposed, and the barriers we have made between ourselves and God begin to crumble. We may well resist the pain involved, but if we are willing to pass through 'the wall' it will become a time of healing, forgiveness, acceptance by God and awareness of his unconditional love. Stillness and silence may become part of our journey.

- **The journey outward:** Faith is now surrendering to God more fully. Drawn closer to him through his unconditional love, we have a renewed sense of calling and ministry. Working from a place of rest within ourselves, we are energized to focus now on the needs of others but from a place of selfless love, not desire for success.

- **The life of love:** Faith is now reflecting God as we begin to see Christ formed within us and live in total obedience to his will. Wisdom that we have gained on the journey is used to help others, and we have a greater detachment from material things and are freed from the stressful striving for position and power of earlier stages. There is a greater contentment about us and we are genuinely compassionate towards others.

Hagberg and Guelich are quick to point out that these stages are very fluid and that there is a lot of movement between them. They also describe how we can get stuck at any particular stage and identify some of the factors that cause us to move on. What is interesting from our point of view is that the two writers clearly point out the need for spiritual mentoring, particularly if we are to move from stage 3 onwards, and crucially when we are facing 'the wall'.

It seems to me that the more goal-oriented churches have something of a vested interest in keeping their members at the 'productive life' stage. One of the reasons they may not welcome an emphasis on spiritual formation and the development of the inner life is because they need busy and active people, staffing the many programmes and projects they have put in place. In developing our church life we have often created a machine that needs to be serviced, and we need people to make the operation run smoothly. We cannot allow them time and space to follow their journey with God. Without consciously realizing it, the church itself may be one of the biggest barriers to a radical pursuit of God.

What we see here also raises questions for church leaders about how we manage the spiritual journeys of individuals when we are responsible for a whole congregation of people. How much can we focus on the specific and personal needs of individuals, and how much should we concentrate on the more general needs of the whole body of Christ? So many discipleship programmes assume that everyone is at the same stage and needs the same help, but is this so? How can we incorporate into our Christian education the insights of the spiritual formation movement? How can we respect the reality of the individual's journey?

It may also raise issues for those in theological education and ministerial training. How can we help students undergoing training with their own personal growth? And how can we ensure that they have a good enough grasp of what is involved in spiritual formation so they can tap into the growing hunger among church members and society at large for a vibrant and relevant spirituality? The same is true for those who prepare and care for our cross-cultural workers. How can we ensure their continued enjoyment of God and their spiritual maturing once they move into demanding ministry situations? How can we equip them so their time of service does not leave them spiritually drained and malnourished?

None of the models we have shared would claim to be the last word on spiritual growth patterns, and all would suggest that whatever stages or phases they describe, life is never as tidy or predictable as abstract schemes suggest. They are at best generalizations, but they do serve a valuable purpose. They can help us identify not only where we are on the journey, but also where other people are, remembering that 'all journeys are similar; but all journeys are different'.[5]

The 'road maps' I have outlined are primarily for the use of those who guide others. It can actually be unhelpful to place a particular model in front of someone and say, 'Look, this is where you are, and this is what's happening to you.' When I am working with individuals, I find it helpful to keep in the back of mind an idea of what the Christian journey looks like. I use different models for different people, but the questions I am always asking myself are: 'Where is this person on their journey?', 'How does what is happening to them reflect the stage at which they are?' and 'How is the Spirit at work to move them on towards the next stage?' I can then use the insights I gain to help the person see for themselves the way forward.

─────── *Chapter Nine* ───────

Roadside assistance:
Some of the key issues

It was a dark, cold, wet and windy evening and I was travelling back from the south of England to my home in the north. The journey homewards meant skirting London on the M25, Britain's busiest motorway. It was rush hour, and every lane on the highway was packed with people hurrying to get to their destinations. Then it happened—the red warning light on the dashboard lit up. I knew I had no alternative but to pull over on to the motorway hard shoulder and phone for help. It was a lonely and dangerous place to be, but fortunately I belong to an organization that provides road-side assistance for breakdowns, and it wasn't too long before help arrived. How glad I was to see the van bearing assistance draw up alongside me! The man's friendly presence brought reassurance and the skilled help I needed.

That incident reminds me of the ministry of the Holy Spirit. In John's Gospel he is called the Comforter or Counsellor, but the Greek word used there (*paracletos*) actually describes someone who 'comes alongside to give aid' (John 14:26; 15:26; 16:7). The Holy Spirit does for us on our spiritual journey what the roadside assist-ance did for me on my homeward journey. He comes alongside us at moments of need to give us comfort, counsel and help. Gently he guides us into the truth which we most need to understand at that particular moment (John 16:13). The Holy Spirit is the true Spiritual Mentor, and he is always with us, and always coming to our aid— but he often ministers to us through other people. Spiritual mentors are those who seek to co-operate with the Spirit in the process of coming alongside God's pilgrim people.

A wide range of needs and situations cause people to seek out the help of a mentor. 'What they have in common,' says experienced spiritual director Peter Ball, 'is that they are aware of a strong urge to go deeper, to take seriously their quest for meaning in life or to find help on their journey of faith in God.'[1] Instinctively we look for a companion to journey with us, someone with whom we can share our story. In those moments when the road seems hard or lonely or we are unsure which road to take, it is reassuring to have another person alongside us. For simplicity, I have grouped some of the main issues that arise in a mentoring context around three main headings: growth, groans and guidance. These words just about sum up the agenda for spiritual mentoring, and we will look at each area in turn.

The desire for growth

Growth is a natural outcome of a healthy spiritual life. We are exhorted by the apostle Peter to 'grow in the grace and knowledge of our Lord and Saviour Jesus Christ' (2 Peter 3:18). The implication is that we can never say we have arrived. There is always something more to learn, something new to experience of the immeasurable love of God. The Holy Spirit continues to create in us a hunger and thirst after righteousness and so, like Paul, we keep pressing on to take hold of that for which Christ Jesus took hold of us (Philippians 3:12). A desire for a growing intimacy with God often surfaces in our lives, and may remain unmet in churches that are activity-led. The pull towards inwardness, which is a natural stage in spiritual growth, is what draws many to seek a spiritual mentor, sometimes outside their own church tradition.

Certainly this was true in my own case. Converted as a teenager, I quickly became involved in church, went to Bible school, became a church leader and served overseas as a missionary. I guess I was in the 'productive life' stage for almost 30 years, and I didn't realize there was anything else. Then God began to create in me a desire for intimacy with him. It came about in two ways. First, I began to see how many Christian workers like myself ended up burnt out, and it frightened me because I knew that I, too, was often living on the edge of exhaustion. I began to think that there must be a better way to live the Christian life than the way I was experiencing. Second, God brought across my path people and books that spoke about a more contemplative approach to living, and I began to hunger for a greater depth in my relationship with God. This took me well beyond my comfort zone, and I began to explore outside my evangelical and charismatic world. This was when God brought me into contact with a woman who became a mentor to me in my search for God, opening up new ways of meeting with God and hearing him speak to me.

I meet many people who are on a similar journey, and it seems to reflect a particular work of the Holy Spirit at this time. There is definitely a growing hunger for a more vital relationship with God among those who have been actively serving him for many years. It is as if we are waking up to the fact that the Christian life is not just about doing things for God but also about knowing him deeply and intimately. As spiritual mentors it will be our privilege to point people towards such a relationship. This will mean introducing them to some of the spiritual disciplines that help us to engage with God more deeply—the practice of stillness, the value of silence and the importance of solitude, for instance. We will be able to guide them into a more reflective way of living, perhaps with the help of journalling, or remind them of the joy of meditating on scripture as a way of getting the truth from our heads to our hearts. We will be able to introduce them to different ways of experiencing God.[2] As we listen to them in their search, we can lead them into the life-changing discovery of our true identity as God's beloved children— an identity not based upon performance or productivity, but made secure because we are in Christ and because God's love is truly unconditional.

For some people, spiritual growth will show itself in dis-satisfaction with their prayer life, and this will cause them to seek out the advice and help of more seasoned travellers. Some will admit that they find prayer difficult. Others will have questions about the very nature of prayer, and how it works or, in some cases, apparently doesn't. Many of us have been schooled in a way of praying that centres around petition and intercession, that is, asking God for our own needs and those of others. There is nothing wrong with this approach to prayer, of course, but there are other aspects to prayer that will take us deeper in our own relationship with God.

A key discovery for many is the insight that prayer is affected by our personality, and therefore the advice 'pray as you can, not as you can't'[3] comes as a liberating truth. The introduction to con-templative prayer provides a vital breakthrough for some. It takes the onus from us in thinking that we somehow have to advise God about what he should be doing. We can simply hold people and situations before him in wordless trust that he is in control. It also reminds us to focus on the Giver rather than the gifts, to be less concerned about what God can do for us and more concerned about loving him for his own sake. In this way prayer moves into a deeper place, into the realm of communion and no longer operates only at the level of request.

Another growth factor is the longing that many have for a more balanced approach to Christian living. Again, as people come to the end of the 'productive life stage', they are feeling more and more the burden of being involved in so many different activities and yet feel guilty whenever they slow down. 'How can I develop a better rhythm in my life?' is a common question asked of spiritual mentors, and it often marks the transition from living outwardly to living from within. We will be able to explore with such people the true meaning of sabbath rest, and how to build time into our busy schedules when we can simply 'be' without the constant pressure to do something.

The very time we give to them can become much-needed 'sacred space' for those for whom life is hectic.

We might be able to introduce them to the practice of regular quiet days or the value of spiritual retreats. We would certainly want to look together at how Jesus balanced his life and lived out of a place of dependency upon the Father. We might consider the whole issue of 'living from within' as the key to effective and efficient Christian living (see, for example, 1 Corinthians 15:10; Galatians 2:20; Colossians 1:29; Philippians 2:12–13; 1 Thessalonians 5:24 and Hebrews 13:20–21). We could explore, too, some of the root causes of workaholism, how to establish personal boundaries, and of course, learning to say 'no'.

The pain of our groans

We have said already that spiritual mentoring is not the same as counselling, but there are some blurred edges, of course, and people often seek the help of a mentor because they are in spiritual pain. A wise mentor will concentrate on issues that affect a person's relationship with God and will approach situations from this perspective. They will also know when they are out of their depth and there is a need to recommend professional counselling, but mentors cannot avoid meeting people in their pain and hearing their 'groans'.

We have spoken already about the experience of hitting what Hagberg and Guelich called 'the wall' (see page 77). This is a very painful transition point in someone's spiritual journey, when the old way of living is being dismantled and a new way of living is being put in place. It will often involve dealing with issues from the past, facing our fears and allowing our wounds to be healed. Mentors can offer at such a time a reassuring, non-judgmental presence and provide the hope that there is a way through and light at the end of the tunnel. We can simply be there for people, validating their experience at a time of confusion and uncertainty, and letting them know they have not lost their way. It is perhaps the moment when the analogy of the spiritual mentor as a midwife comes in to play—we are watching something being born, but giving birth is painful and slow!

Some will seek help because they are aware of failure, and they need a safe place where they can admit their need for forgiveness and restoration. This brings a sacramental role to spiritual mentoring, for the hearing of confession and the application of forgiving grace are priestly functions which have been given to us all (see John 20:21–23; James 5:16). The hardest thing for many people to do after they have fallen is to forgive themselves. They know in their heads that God forgives them but cannot feel it in their hearts. Such people usually need to hear the reassuring words 'You are forgiven' from another human being before the truth sinks in and sets them free. It is a great privilege to be entrusted with the confession of another person, and we must treat their disclosure with the greatest care and sensitivity and, of course, confidentiality.

Another group of people will want to talk about the pain of their disappointments, their shattered dreams, or what they might see as broken promises.[4] Many grow up with simplistic formulas for successful Christian living. They have God in a box and feel they can predict how he will work. When the outcome isn't what they expect, they are bewildered. One common formula that people live by is that 'obedience equals blessing, disobedience equals lack of blessing'. It can sound very biblical, especially in the light of some Old Testament passages, and for a time it may seem to work. Eventually, however, some age-old question of faith will arise, creating a crisis of confidence: why do the wicked prosper? Why do good things happen to bad people?

Tom had given his whole life to Christian service, and the motto 'those who honour me I will honour' (1 Samuel 2:30) had always been his watchword. He reasoned therefore that if he and his wife put God first in their lives, their children would naturally follow them in the faith. When eventually his children turned their backs on God, Tom was confounded. It seemed that God had let him down big time, and inside he felt very angry with God. He learned to live with his pain and continued in ministry but with a lot of resentment towards God. It was only when talking with his mentor that his pain rose to the surface and he was able to express his frustration and hurt. To his surprise his mentor questioned the very watchword that he had been living by and asked him to think about it more deeply. Tom took the question back to God. Had he really been living by a false premise all these years? Gradually he realized what he had done. He had subtly introduced his own terms into the agreement he had with God. He had in fact made a bargain with God, and he realized that he had reduced God to a formula and boxed him into a way of acting that he in his own wisdom had determined. While in general the premise that God honours those who honour him is true, Tom saw that he could not determine in what way God should honour him. As he looked at his life and ministry, he could see that God had indeed blessed him in many ways, beyond what he deserved. He still feels the pain of his children's being away from God, but his animosity towards God has disappeared and his understanding of God has been enlarged.

Church leaders in particular need someone to talk to about their pain. Very often there will be no one within their congregations with whom they can be open and honest about their own struggles, so an outside reference point can be a lifesaver to those caught up in the pressures of ministry. Those in 'full-time' Christian work face their own particular stresses and temptations, and the opportunity to talk through relevant issues of ministry with someone who understands can act as a safety valve. The same applies to the spouses of church leaders. Missionaries face similar struggles. Often placed on a pedestal by others, they can feel isolated and lonely on their own journey. One senior missionary said to me recently, 'I've been in this mission most of my life, and I've had countless appraisals, but it's always been about the work. No one has ever said to me, "David, how are you? How is it with your soul?"'

There are two other aspects of pain that we will commonly encounter, and both are so important that we will devote a separate chapter to each (see Chapters 10 and 11). The first of these is the 'groan' of questions about faith, the painful heart-searching many experience as they move into a more adult expression of faith. The other is the 'groan' of the dark night of the soul, that period when we lose track of God and all sense of his presence.

The need for guidance

The value of having a soul friend or mentor is often most keenly felt in times of change and transition when the need for companion-ship on the journey is acute. Likewise, moments when we have key life decisions to make can be occasions to seek out the objective counsel of a trusted friend or guide, someone whose advice we respect and who will help us to weigh up all the options and possibilities.

One lesson I have learned over the years is that the will of God is actually a very broad place. I used to think that guidance was like walking a tightrope—there was only one possible way to go, and if you made the wrong choice you fell off into God's second best. This meant that for me (and for many others) guidance was always a stressful business, because you could easily get it wrong and miss your way, which might prove disastrous. I now realize that we can be much more relaxed about guidance because God is committed to revealing his will to us and to helping us walk in his ways. In fact the responsibility for guidance lies with him, and he is well able to make his will perfectly clear to us. For our part, the key ingredient is to place ourselves in the position where we can be led by the Spirit. It is more about preparing our hearts, offering ourselves to him for whatever he wants, and then doing what seems right. As long as we truly want to please God, we can trust our hearts to guide us.

Some will have been brought up with a mistrust of their own desires, concluding that if we really want to do something, it must be wrong, because it is likely to be us who want it and not God. Another way of looking at it, though, is to recognize that our deepest desires have been placed there by God, and as we uncover and respond to them, we are in fact discovering the will of God. In creating us, God has placed his own desires into our hearts. It is part of the way he has made us, how he has uniquely shaped us, and we do his will by becoming the people he made us to be and daring to live from our hearts. This is confirmed by Psalm 37:4 (NRSV): 'Take delight in the Lord, and he will give you the desires of your heart.' In good Ignatian tradition, one of the tasks of a mentor will be to help an individual uncover the true desire of their heart and then respond to it.

People will instinctively be drawn to a mentor when they are in the process of transition, leaving one phase of life and about to enter another. This will often centre upon a possible career change or development in ministry. We have seen how important these transitions are from Clinton's stages of leadership development and, not surprisingly, those involved in ministry will often want to talk through where the next phase of the journey might take them. Weighing up the pros and cons of possible moves requires the process of discernment we have spoken about already, and having someone to accompany us as we work through that process can be a great help.

One group in particular who will appreciate the help of a spiritual mentor is that of those missionaries who are returning to their home countries after living abroad. This is a major transition and often proves to be a turbulent time for even the most resourceful of individuals. Alison Palmer, a spiritual director from New Zealand, suggests several ways by which we can help people navigate the currents of cross-cultural re-entry:[5]

- Be there to listen and point the person to God so they have a spiritual perspective on all that is happening.
- Be there through the process of transition (it can take as long as two years), walking with them on the slow journey.
- Encourage reflection on the past, and the integration of the lessons learned into the present and the future.
- Help them to grieve for what is past, and to face the realities of the present, while having hope for the future.
- Help with the process of discernment in the many choices that have to be made.

It is easy to see why people value the ministry of spiritual mentoring so highly. We all need people to inspire us and call us on to greater things, people who will share with us from their experience and help us to grow. Sometimes we need a listening ear, someone to share our troubles with, a shoulder to lean on when we feel hard pressed, a shelter in the time of storm. Occasionally we will want someone to walk with us through our times of uncertainty or to help us choose wisely in moments of opportunity.

It was God who said, 'It is not good for the man to be alone' (Genesis 2:18), and Solomon who wisely recognized that 'two are better than one' (Ecclesiastes 4:9). Spiritual mentoring is vital because it meets the deeply felt need in each of us for spiritual companionship.

✣

—————— *Chapter Ten* ——————

Losing the way:
Mentoring those with questions of faith

I recently got lost on the London Underground. While I am fairly familiar with how the system works, I was in a section that I had never used before, and my journey required me to change lines at a busy interchange that was new to me. It was rush hour, and although I thought I had followed the directions carefully, I ended up hopelessly lost and disorientated, going round in circles. I was due to catch another train from the mainline station, and time was running out. I began to panic and to feel hot and bothered and annoyed with myself. It's not a nice feeling, being lost! Then, suddenly, and I'm not sure how, I picked up the signs again, found the right platform and caught the train just in time. What a relief!

One of the main entry points into spiritual mentoring is the need that many people have to explore where they are in terms of their faith journey, and to be able to ask questions which might otherwise be considered risky in a safe context. In some sense they have lost their way. Alan Jamieson, a New Zealand Baptist minister, has highlighted the fact that significant numbers of people with a background in evangelical, Pentecostal and charismatic churches are dropping out of church, or 'jumping ship' as he calls it.[1] They are not the only ones, of course, but it is perhaps a little surprising to see this happening in what has previously been considered a very stable section of the church. My own experience bears witness to this trend. Not only do I have friends who have dropped out, but in my work as a retreat leader and training consultant I regularly meet people in a similar position. Further, there are those who, for various reasons, stay in church but find it increasingly irrelevant and unsatisfying. They are the 'internal leavers' and they live one step from the door. Mentors need to be aware of this particular group of people and understand how to help them in their pain.

Jamieson identifies four categories of church leavers:

- The disillusioned followers, who leave because they are either hurt or angry. These probably stop attending church but maintain their belief system, finding support in groups and events outside church structures.
- The reflective exiles, who, because of crises or intellectual problems, question the faith they have received and want time away from church to think matters through before they decide what they really believe.
- The transitional explorers, who want to find a new way forward and are open to change and new ideas which are quite different from what they once held. They may become more liberal in their beliefs and even leave the Christian faith altogether.
- The integrated wayfarers, who have questioned their faith and put it all back together again in a new way. They are ready to journey on again, albeit with a very different mindset.

One of the ways Jamieson suggests we can understand what is happening to these people is by using the model of faith development suggested by James Fowler. I did not include this in Chapter 8, 'Road maps and guidebooks', because it fits better here and comes from a slightly different perspective, but it is a useful tool for understanding why people with firmly held beliefs can have a crisis of faith, and why those of previously strong convictions can apparently lose their way.

Fowler's outline looks like this, and emphasizes how we believe, not what we believe:

- **Stage 1—The innocent:** the pre-school years with experience of God understood through family experience and without any personal inner structure.
- **Stage 2—The literalist:** from six years old onwards, with ideas and stories taken literally. About 20 per cent of adults stay at this stage, with a strong literalist interpretation of the Bible and a faith built around rules and regulations.
- **Stage 3—The loyalist:** a conformist period where we are acutely attuned to the expectations of others and where beliefs are deeply held but not critically examined. This is the most common stage for adult churchgoers.
- **Stage 4—The critic:** a new examination of beliefs and expectations leading to the development of an independent position.
- **Stage 5—The seer:** this stage is seldom reached before midlife and involves a new openness to mystery and other broader perspectives, with faith integrated into the whole of life.
- **Stage 6—The saint:** self is removed from the centre of focus, and there is a complete acceptance of the authority of God in all aspects of life.

We immediately see some points of connections with other 'road maps', but the big difference here is the way in which faith grows and develops through questioning and being open to new things. For faith to become strong and genuine it must in some sense be made our own, so that we can operate out of our own convictions. It must arise from within, rather than be imposed from without. Such a transition may indeed be a rough passage, and the help of a trusted guide will prove invaluable. Anyone who wants to grow and mature in their faith beyond stage 3 will have to go through stages 4 and 5, and this is the period when they are likely to drop out of church, at least for a while.

Jane found herself at such a point of transition. As a student she had been deeply involved in the life of a charismatic house church, which at first had been very helpful but later became controlling.

Questions were discouraged, conformity was required, and the tight bonding of the members made it hard to leave. Eventually, when her husband moved into full-time Christian work, they were able to move on, but her struggle with faith continued. She had many questions, especially about the Old Testament, and gradually God began to seem unreal and distant, and faith a cruel illusion. One day she realized she could no longer believe or be committed. Over the next two years she dropped out of all church activities and struggled to attend at all.

Eventually, with her husband's help, she began to talk with a trusted spiritual mentor. The abusive nature of her church experience became clearer, and with the help of a professional counsellor she worked through some of the issues raised. She was encouraged to read more widely and discovered that others were asking similar questions and that there were credible Christian alternatives to the simplistic faith that had failed her so spectacularly. Healing began to take place and a slow recovery of faith. Then, in her own words, came a 'moment of grace': 'One night, without ceremony, I simply began to talk to God. And he, without ceremony, came and listened —and spoke. I felt the presence I remembered and knew that God was there.'

Jane began to attend church again, although with a different perspective. She still struggles with church and finds evangelical certainty hard to bear. 'One thing I am certain of,' she says, 'is that God has got hold of my life. I believe I am on a journey, although I do not know the destination. I do have faith in Jesus, but I need to keep asking questions. I want to explore what my renewed faith means. It is not the same as I held before, but I am on board again.'

Jane's experience is typical of many and helps us to understand the growing pains of developing a mature faith. How then can we mentor those who come to us and who are disillusioned, disenchanted or disorientated? Well, clearly we will need to allow people to ask their questions and explore their own thoughts so that they can arrive at their own answers. We must not try to impose our beliefs on them or feel that we have to defend the church or maintain the status quo. We ourselves must be comfortable with questions, doubts and even denials. We will need to listen with bags of patience and loads of understanding, for it takes time for people to process things, and there may well be a lot of anger about. Further, we can help people in specific areas.

Our idea of God

Very often the reason for disillusionment with church has to do with faulty concepts of God which have been inherited. Such people may carry in their minds an idea of a God who is always angry, increasingly demanding, unfair or unjust, even in some ways cruel. We may want to explore where such ideas came from. We will certainly want to try to direct them through the scriptures to a more wholesome understanding of God—a holy God of love, a gracious heavenly Father, a Good Shepherd who cares for us, and so on.

The grace of God

I have been amazed how many Christians have never truly entered into an experience of grace. The reason why many find church such a burden is that they live with the weight of legalism on their shoulders. Gently exposing this basic distortion of the Christian gospel will bring relief, and opening up to them a proper understanding of the gospel of grace will bring liberty and an altogether different appreciation for the faith.

The rhythm of life

Another reason why people become disenchanted with church is that they do not know how to live balanced lives, and they become overwhelmed and exhausted with trying to do everything and please everyone. We can help them to value and appreciate the need for sabbath rest and to establish boundaries for themselves. We can show them how to work out priorities, to prune their diaries, and to make time for leisure without feeling guilty. It's remarkable how our perspective on life can change when we are properly rested.

Relationship issues and the question of forgiveness

When people have been badly hurt through abusive church situations, their pain will need to be validated, and they may well need emotional healing. They will need to be 'heard' for what they have been through, and their concerns truly acknowledged. For their own sakes they may need to forgive those who have hurt them so they are not imprisoned by bitterness, even if reconciliation is not possible.

Finding God in the desert of experience

The metaphor of the desert is one that Jamieson uses to describe what it feels like to be in this situation.[2] It can seem that God is silent, absent or disinterested. We know, of course, that God can be found even in the desert and there is plenty of scriptural encouragement to believe that he will come to us even there (see, for example, Deuteronomy 32:10–12). We can explore with them such questions as, 'How can I live here? How can I grow here? What am I to learn here?'

Travelling companions

This part of the journey can seem very lonely but there are in fact many pilgrims out there whose journey will be similar. Travelling companions often show up in unlikely places. Increasingly support groups are coming into being, and through the Internet it is possible to join discussion groups where questions can be explored and ideas shared.[3] A spiritual mentor might even gather a group together of those he or she feels are at a similar point in their journey.

A group of spiritual mentors from New Zealand was asked the question, 'What do church leavers need in their own deserts of faith?' From their own experience of interacting with such a group, they highlighted the following key points:

- A safe, non-judgmental place where our experience can be validated and we can explore beyond the 'safe' and the known.
- Assurance that this is a time of God, not of the devil or personal failure; some anchors and handholds; the chance to learn more about the desert and the dark night.
- Support for our grief and loss, encouragement to trust our own wisdom, help in creating new boundaries; companionship and friendship in the hard places.
- Permission to rest and take a break from frenetic Christian activity.

To walk with others during their 'wilderness wanderings' is a challenging but rewarding experience. It is a privilege to be taken into the confidence of someone who has the courage to explore their faith, to challenge the known and the safe, and to be open to change and redirection. We do not need to have all the answers, and we will not be able to assuage all the pain—but we can be there for such weary travellers and give them the gift of our hospitality.

❖

Chapter Eleven

Travelling by night: When God seems absent

If ever I have to drive to an unfamiliar place, I much prefer, if I can, to make the journey during the daytime. Driving at night is much more difficult, and it's so easy to lose your way when you can't see the road signs properly and are not sure where you should be going anyway! Travelling by night is no fun.

All of us have periods of darkness in our lives, moments of despair or doubt when we feel we might be losing our way. The crises of life touch us all, and we may feel that we have been abandoned by God, and that we are on our own. It feels as if God has hidden his face from us—a common complaint in the Old Testament. Normally such experiences do not last too long, and we quickly recover. There is another experience of spiritual darkness, however, for which there seems to be no apparent reason, and which feels as if it will go on for ever. This has traditionally been known as the 'dark night of the soul', and is the second major cause of pain among God's people that we need to be aware of as spiritual mentors, and to which we will be called upon to respond.

The experience of the dark night is not often acknowledged among evangelical and charismatic believers. The assumption generally seems to be that if we are living the 'victorious life' we should not really be experiencing such 'down' times. The normal advice given to anyone who may feel they are experiencing spiritual darkness is that they should pull themselves together and get on with it; it is a question of either 'grin and bear it' or of 'pulling your socks up'.

However, other sections of the church have long recognized the dark night as a valid part of the Christian journey, and indeed as a mark of maturity and progress in God, not a sign of weakness.

It is to St Teresa of Avila (1515–82) and St John of the Cross (1542–91) that we look for explanation about the dark night. Both of them saw the Christian life as a journey upwards into union with God, with the dark night being the prelude to the fullest experience of intimacy with God. Both write very symbolically. As Gordon Mursell describes it: 'John's spiritual path is a lover's journey at night, in darkness, up the slopes of Mount Carmel. "Night" is a complex symbol: it means exciting mystery, the bare faith, the pain and detachment, that accompany the journey.'[1]

The dark night is clearly not a fun place to be. We all have our ups and downs, but this is different. Russell Metcalfe describes the experience as well as anyone: 'The dark night is something else. The lights go out. The screens go black. The lines are dead. God is not answering his phone. And as hard as we look, there is no light at the end of the tunnel. Where is God now?'[2] This experience of God's absence is felt most painfully by those who have been most aware of his presence. Suddenly to lose all sense of God, to be bereft of the emotional awareness of his presence, is both bewildering and baffling, especially when it seems that there is no discernible reason for it to happen. 'There are times,' says Alexander Ryrie, 'when a person is overwhelmed by an experience of darkness or emptiness, when God seems distant and prayer becomes impossible... God withdraws and darkness comes upon them for no apparent reason, and no amount of seeking or attempted prayer brings his return.'[3]

Is such an experience grounded in biblical reality, or it is the product of mystical imagination? We have mentioned already the cry of the Psalmist when God apparently hides his face, not because we have sinned, but for some reason known only to himself: 'How long, O Lord? Will you forget me for ever? How long will you hide your face from me? How long must I wrestle with my thoughts and every day have sorrow in my heart?' (Psalm 13:1–2, and see also

10:1; 27:9; 44:24; 88:13–14; 89:46; 143:7). It would seem that God's people frequently had the sense that God was hiding his presence from them. The prophet Isaiah seems to recognize the problem, too, when he says, 'Let him who walks in the dark, who has no light, trust in the name of the Lord and rely on his God' (Isaiah 50:10). Perhaps we catch a glimpse of the dark night also in the 'Shepherd Psalm', which appears to assume we will at some stage 'walk through the valley of deep darkness' (Psalm 23:4, literal translation).

The life stories of some of the great Bible characters also reveal the reality of this experience. We think of Elijah, fleeing in terror from Jezebel, and coping at the same time with the physical and emotional exhaustion following his confrontation with the priests of Baal on Mount Carmel. Tired and weary, the mighty man of God retires into the cave and sinks into a dark night of his own where he feels completely abandoned, even by his God. Certainty and confidence have been replaced by doubt and confusion, and he despairs of life itself (see 1 Kings 19:1–9). Or what about Job and his struggle of faith? Not only does he pass through a period of great trial when all he holds dear is taken from him, but in the aftermath he has to endure this same sense of abandonment by God. 'Yet when I looked for good,' he says, 'evil came; when I looked for light, then came darkness' (Job 30:26). In addition, he has to endure the misguided advice of his friends who can interpret his sufferings only through the inadequate grid of their own theology. Surely he has brought this upon himself? All counsellors should note that there are times when understanding silence and accepting presence are far better responses than condemning voices, empty words and meaningless clichés. Job, however, refuses to give up or to let go of his faith. He cries out to God and speaks honestly from his pain and confusion, but he never turns his back on God. At the end of the drama, none of the characters, including Job, could understand it all. The 'why' remained something of a mystery to them. They simply stood in silence and awe before the true majesty and mystery of a God whose ways are sometimes beyond our understanding (Romans 11:33–35).

It is interesting to note that both Elijah and Job are commended to us in the New Testament as examples to follow, Job for his patience (James 5:10–11) and Elijah for his shared humanity and prayerfulness (vv. 17–18). We could add to our list, too, the apostle Peter, who, following his denial of Jesus, appears to have endured his own dark night of the soul—a period when, as Jesus predicted, his soul was sifted like wheat (Luke 22:31–32, 61–62).

The greatest validation of the dark night experience, however, is surely given to us in the sufferings of Jesus in Gethsemane and on the cross. Jesus' dark night began in Gethsemane as he was first let down by his disciples, then betrayed by Judas, and finally deserted by everyone (Matthew 26:36–56). Alone he faced the agonizing choice to drink the cup of suffering, and alone he faced the ridicule of the Sanhedrin and the abuse of the soldiers as he was wrongly condemned to death. Then, as he is crucified, darkness covers the whole land, as if symbolic of his inner spiritual desolation. 'My God, my God, why have you forsaken me?' (Matthew 27:46) is his painful cry as he tastes for the first time what it means to feel deserted by the Father. Jesus is our example in all things. If he learned obedience through what he suffered (Hebrews 5:8), why should we be spared? If this is the path the Master trod, should not the servant tread it as well?

If we can accept that there is a biblical warrant for recognizing the reality of a spiritual experience such as the dark night, we are left with the question, 'What is it for?' What is a God of love doing when he withdraws the sense of his presence from us? Remember, we are not talking here of the kind of separation which is brought about by our own sinfulness (Isaiah 59:2) nor by an experience of crisis, loss or bereavement. This is something much deeper, which lasts longer and affects us far more profoundly but which is allowed by God for a purpose. It does not mean that God is displeased with us. Someone has compared it to the experience of Jonah when he is caught in the darkness of the belly of the whale. It feels as if you are going nowhere, but in fact God is carrying you in the darkness to the place where he wants you to be. A dark night is taking us where we need to go, even though we think we are going in the wrong direction.

To some extent mystery is part of knowing God, because we can never know him fully. Indeed, our sense that God is absent might just be because he is actually there, and we are so close to him that we are overshadowed by him. The very nearness of God could be the cause of the darkness. What appears to be dark could actually be the blindness that comes as we draw closer to the light. 'He made darkness his covering, his canopy around him,' says David (Psalm 18:11) , describing an encounter he had with God. In some way God veils his presence for our sake. At the dedication of the temple, the Lord's presence so filled the place that the priests could not perform their duties because of the cloud. Solomon explained what happened like this: 'The Lord has said that he would dwell in a dark cloud' (1 Kings 8:10–13). Clearly darkness should not be automatically equated with God's absence.

There is a very real sense in which God is actually paying us the greatest compliment when he allows the dark night to come upon us, because he is entrusting us with an experience not many could bear. This is not for those in the early stages of the faith pilgrimage; it is for those who are at graduate school and who truly desire intimacy with God. From one perspective we could say that God is calling us into the fellowship of sharing in the sufferings of Jesus (Philippians 3:10–11). We are able to feel to some small degree what he felt as he suffered on our behalf, and as we identify ourselves with him, we begin to become even more like him in our thoughts and attitudes and in submission to the will of the Father. It is the oneness of lovers who gladly share everything together, the rough and the smooth, and who become closer because of what they have been through. Perhaps this explains why it is often those with the greatest love for God who are called to walk this difficult path.

There is no doubt, too, that the dark night is a period of intense purification when we are weaned away from the material things of the world, allowed to see our own sinfulness and begin to realize our great love for God. There is a saying that 'absence makes the heart grow fonder', and certainly the withdrawal of the tangible sense of God's nearness only makes the believer long for him even more. Compared to the joy of knowing and experiencing God's love, all else is worthless. This is what we realize in the dark night. The soul is filled with an intense hunger and thirst for God. 'My soul thirsts for you,' says the psalmist; 'my flesh faints for you, as in a dry and weary land where there is no water' (Psalm 63:1, NRSV; see also 42:2; 143:6). The dark night is often the precursor of blessing to come, the gateway into a deeper union with God.

I think we can also say that in allowing such an experience to come our way, God is strengthening us and teaching us to walk by faith and not by sight (2 Corinthians 5:7). When all evidence of God's presence seems to be gone from our lives, we are left with 'naked' faith, and we simply have to trust that he is there, even though we have no evidence to prove it. This is the purest kind of faith; it is the faith that says with Job, 'Though he slay me, yet will I hope in him' (Job 13:15) and again, 'He knows the way that I take; when he has tested me I shall come forth as gold' (Job 23:10; see also 1 Peter 1:7). Satan, of course, cannot accept that a human being could love God for his own sake. He believes that people love God only for what they can get from him. Job's story proves that this is not always so.

While we can make some suggestions as to what God may be doing at such a period, we know we are on the edge of mystery and our words must be filled with caution. We do not always understand God's ways, and learning to live with this 'unknowing' is part of our growth. As wise mentors we will be slow to make pronouncements about how we interpret what is happening in the life of another at such a time. We can, however, help to guide them through the darkness with some practical advice, offered sensitively and at the appropriate time.

Something said by many who have experienced the dark night is that it is better not to fight it but to go with it. Certainly there are times when it is right to resist negative circumstances, but if we detect that it is in fact God who is at work, then we do better to submit to his gracious dealings with us. This doesn't mean being passive, however. We will want to stand steady at such a time, as Job did, to hold our nerve and keep trusting in God. We will want to fix our eyes on Jesus (Hebrews 12:1–3) and to continue to praise God despite our feelings (Psalm 34:1–3).

Something practical which may help is to take physical exercise so we are tired out at the end of the day and can then rest better. There is much mental and emotional turmoil during the dark night and sleep may not come easily. As Elijah discovered, sleep can be profoundly restorative, and simply having a good night's rest can make a world of difference to our ability to cope with what we are going through.

It is important at such a time to be honest with God and, perhaps through journalling, tell him frankly what we are feeling and thinking, in the knowledge that he can cope with the outpouring of our anger and frustration. It is important to be honest with others as well, and talking to friends whom we trust is also very healing. Not all will understand, though, and not all will be able to cope with something as baffling as a dark night experience, so we must choose wisely with whom we share. Again, we see the value of an established mentoring relationship, and the blessing of having someone to walk alongside us no matter what is happening.

Finally, we can wait patiently for the Lord. One of the desert fathers, Isaac of Nineveh, put it well when he gave this advice: 'Wrap your head in your cloak and sleep, until the hour of darkness is over, but do not leave your cell.' When we realize that times of darkness are normal parts of the process by which we are led closer to God, we need not panic or be afraid. We can put our hope in God, believing that the clouds will part and the sun will shine again. Darkness does not last for ever, and eventually it will pass. We can share David's optimism: 'I am still confident of this: I will see the goodness of the Lord in the land of the living. Wait for the Lord; be strong and take heart and wait for the Lord' (Psalm 27:13–14).

It has often been noted that the dark night usually occurs at times of transition and significant spiritual growth. As I reflect on this, I see a connection with the stages of the 'critical journey' as described by Hagberg and Guelich, and outlined in Chapter 8 (pages 76–78). I think the experience of 'the wall' may come to some people in the form of the dark night, marking their transition from the productive life lived in dependence upon self to the outer journey and the life of love characterized by dependency upon God. When it occurs at this stage, the dark night becomes a place of brokenness, and its effect is well summed up by Bruce Demarest:

For a season, God providentially distances himself, causing light to become darkness. Spiritually God's absence creates a vacuum that can show us the emptiness of our fleshly attachments, such as our dependence on people and things for a security they cannot give and our reliance on position and money for power that is weak indeed... And so, through the anguish of the dark night, God performs something like 'spiritual surgery' on deeply rooted self-sufficiency, sensuality and pride. [4]

The dark night may also occur during stage 6, the 'life of love' as described by Hagberg and Guelich. This is clearly a stage of great maturity, characterized by total obedience to God, detachment from the things of the world, and joyful abandonment to God's will. Their description of a person at this stage seems to fit well with the emptying of self that is an outcome of the dark night:

We have little ambition for being well known, rich, successful, noteworthy, goal-oriented or 'spiritual'. We are like vessels into which God pours his Spirit, constantly overflowing. We are Spirit-filled but in a quiet, un-assuming way. So pervasive is the presence of the Spirit in our lives that we may not even be particularly conscious of doing something of the Spirit.

We are oblivious to the Spirit because we are accustomed to God moving very naturally through our lives, unexpectedly and surely.[5]

If these are the outcomes of the dark night (and I think they are) then, while not actually seeking such an experience, we may be able to welcome it, should God in his wisdom and love decide to grant it. And if we have this understanding for ourselves, we may be able to 'shine the torch' for others, providing them with the word that will be a lamp for their feet and a light for their path at a time when the night may be very dark indeed (Psalm 119:105).

——————— *Chapter Twelve* ———————

Group travel:
Spiritual mentoring in small groups

I often travel to Singapore and the immigration form I am required to fill out always asks the same question: are you travelling alone or in a group? Usually I am alone, but many other people do travel in groups such as organized tour parties, and there's a lot to be said for it. Group travel can be much cheaper, a lot safer, and (given the right companions) great fun.

We have been thinking of the mentoring process in a one-to-one context, but there are very good reasons for integrating it into the setting of a small group. The spiritual life cannot be lived in splendid isolation. It needs to be grounded in the reality of relationships with others. As Robert Bellah has said, 'We never get to the bottom of ourselves on our own. We discover who we are face-to-face and side-by-side with others in work, love and learning.'[1]

The small group has always been the basic unit of spiritual growth, and most churches now see it as an essential part of normal church life. Spiritual mentoring is a labour-intensive ministry and something of a specialized calling. We can try to increase the number of mentors available, but supply is always likely to be outstripped by the demand. By building spiritual mentoring into small group ministry we can make it available more easily and multiply its benefits significantly. Further, the small group setting offers a natural opportunity for people to share their faith stories and meet with others who are on the same path. A smaller number of people makes for greater intimacy, and an informal setting (whether in a home or coffee shop or elsewhere) provides a place of relaxation and welcome that encourages open and honest sharing. What excites me most about mentoring in small groups is that it is perfectly suited to the needs of a younger, postmodern generation.

Younger people today are not unspiritual. In fact, they are very open to spiritual things but they may be suspicious of religious institutions and dogmatic approaches. They want the openness to explore and discuss, to question and discover. They value relationships deeply and want to be connected with others in their search for meaning. They long to be accepted for who they are, to be authentic and real. They are comfortable with ambiguity and not afraid of mystery. Heather Webb, a spiritual director and minister in the US, advocates using small groups to tap into this spiritual need:

We are at a point in history where the longing for faith, for meaning, is on the rise. We are faced with a population hungry for connection, for relationship, for a sense of belonging to something bigger than themselves. If we are willing to rethink our assumptions about faith and the church, we can offer the hungry masses a faith feast of unimaginable proportions.[2]

Small groups that are open to questioning and allow participants to explore their thoughts and feelings are ideal for the kind of people we spoke about in Chapter 10. They may be dissatisfied by church and may have been wounded in the past, and they may be asking difficult and awkward questions, but many would still love to be part of a group in which their searching is respected and welcomed. A warm and accepting group with a focus on spiritual mentoring can provide such wanderers with a safe haven during a stormy time in their faith journey.

David Benner is also a keen advocate of spiritual accompaniment in small groups and describes it as his great hope for the church.[3] He envisages groups that meet, not for Bible study or fellowship, but for the specific purpose of offering spiritual friendship and direction. He suggests that such groups should operate with four basic ideals:

- **The priority of questions over answers**: We should not be afraid of questioning because the spiritual journey inevitably throws up lots of questions for us. Neither should we feel the pressure to have an answer for every question. The church should be a home for seekers as well as finders.
- **Prayerful listening**: The aim is to develop an ethos in which listening to God and to each other becomes natural. Silence will therefore be a significant ingredient as the group seeks to be attentive to God.
- **Sharing spiritual experiences**: Sharing will centre around the participant's experience of God in the midst of their everyday lives, and not just general chit-chat. Often the group will have prepared beforehand by journalling, and they will come to the meeting with something to share about how they perceive God to be working in their lives. Each person may be invited to share while the others listen.
- **A climate of support and acceptance**: Members are not there to offer advice but to listen and give encouragement. They will seek to speak the truth in love, offering any insights they feel may be from God, but in an open-handed way that invites consideration but does not demand acceptance.

How might such a group come into being? Initially it may be started by someone who feels the need for this type of gathering, and the members will be those who share a similar desire for spiritual accompaniment and are willing to support others prayerfully on their journey. A group like this needs a high degree of trust and oneness of purpose, so it may be helpful to agree a group covenant together at the start. Group members will need to commit themselves to an honest relationship with God, wholehearted participation to the group process through prayerful listening and response, and opening their spiritual journeys to the analysis of others. The group needs to be small in size, with a maximum of perhaps six people. Larger groups might start off with an initial time together and then break into smaller units for the listening process. Some groups could be of the same sex (this can make openness easier) or of mixed gender (which gives a different perspective). Diversity is to be encouraged, and differences of age, personality, social standing and such like should not be a barrier.

Someone who has pioneered the use of small groups in this way is Sister Rose Mary Dougherty. She trains both facilitators and potential participants in the process of spiritual direction, and then arranges monthly meetings of the groups. She describes the process like this:

Group spiritual direction is grounded in mystery. We use a very simple process which honours and supports this grounding; silence, the sharing of a participant, silence, response from the group, silence. We repeat the process until all individuals have had time for sharing and response from the group. We add a few minutes on at the end to reflect on our time together. [4]

Fleshed out a little more, the group might work as follows. The meeting begins with shared prayer—either audibly or silently—then, quieting down and intentionally letting go of ordinary busyness, intensity and task orientation. Each participant has half an hour, which is organized in the following way:

- A 15-minute spoken presentation of how they believe they hear and respond to the Lord through prayer, scripture reading, study, worship, other disciplines, life experiences and relationships and service; where they feel they follow the Lord easily and sense God's blessings; where they feel resistant, have questions, seem to be stuck, or God appears 'absent'.

- Two to four minutes of silence, prayer and reflection as group members consider what the Lord might be saying, inviting or asking through what has been presented. They can write down what may be appropriate to say.
- Ten minutes of group feedback and some dialogue. Through affirmation, questions, scripture and the prayerful presence of the group, the presenter is helped in clarifying and discerning the leading of God's Spirit. Refraining from giving advice to 'fix things', we learn to be prayerfully receptive to the Spirit, and thus allow each other to become more centred and dependent on God.
- Two to four minutes of silence, journalling and prayer. Then it is the turn of the next group member and the cycle is repeated.
- When all the group members have had a turn, the group may wish to make some observations about the general qualities and content of their time together, what the Lord seems to be saying to them, and how they did and did not remain prayerfully attentive to each other and the Lord. Often groups choose to close with a few minutes of shared prayer with and for each other, expressing gratitude and intentionally placing whatever seems appropriate into God's care. At times it may seem better to close with shared silent prayer or singing together.

Except for the initial greeting, longer social conversation is saved for the end of the group meeting.

This description is not meant to be prescriptive, and groups will develop their own rhythms and patterns, but it does help to have in our minds how it could function. I have the joy of being part of a group of five church leaders who meet regularly (about every six to eight weeks) for a time of seeking God together. We have no agenda other than encouraging each other in our walk with God. We meet at a nearby retreat centre and, after catching up with personal news over coffee, we spend the rest of the morning in personal quiet during which we journal, read scripture and reflect on our own lives. We then come together for lunch (a social interlude), before sharing with each other in a way similar to that outlined above. It is a key time for each of us. We have being doing this for a few years now, so the level of trust and appreciation for each other is high. Being a group of extraverts, though, we do find the silence part a little challenging!

Heather Webb believes that, given today's spiritual climate and the way this may shape the future of small groups, a leader or facilitator will need new gifts beyond simply being just a good teacher or discussion leader. She suggests that one key development will be to see small group leadership in terms of spiritual direction. In other words, we should give leaders the skills to act as spiritual directors for their groups. She says:

This new era has opened the door for Christians to own our doubt and to stand with others who are asking hard questions of faith and spirituality. Small groups based in spiritual direction provide the church with a rich tool for reaching into the postmodern culture and bringing out its gold. [5]

In fact, the merging of small group ministry and spiritual direction can create a new model for community life. Bible study groups and evangelistic cells have their place, but there is a need for small groups with no other agenda than drawing people closer to God and each other.

Webb helpfully presents us with three possible models for small groups with this character. The first is the *story-centred group*. The church has always been a place of sanctuary for the bruised, the broken and the flawed. Small groups can offer the same protection to their members and their stories. They can become places where people can share their secrets without fear of punishment or judgment. Stories of life and faith are the substance of our journey towards God, and people need a chance to share them. Each meeting centres on one person, who shares three or four scenes from the past that have been defining moments for them. The group then has the opportunity to offer feedback or to ask questions to open up what has been shared. The leader guides the process through and ensures a prayerful responsiveness from the other members.

A second model is the *text-centred group*. Here scripture will be used, but it may not be the only text, and it will be used in a way that reflects the nature of the group as one seeking to listen to God. It may well use an approach like *Lectio Divina* (see Appendix B). This is sometimes described as the contemplative reading of scripture. It means we can hear God speak to us without having to argue over the meaning of the text! The group may also choose to read some of the spiritual classics, discuss contemporary novels or consider film clips. God has a thousand ways of speaking to us, including through our own culture, and we can find his word hidden in many surprising places.

Her third suggestion is for the *prayer-centred group*, which fits most closely with the traditional model for spiritual mentoring. By intentionally creating space and silence, such groups provide a context in which we can hear the voice of God better. Sometimes the group might be entirely given over to contemplative prayer, sometimes it might follow the pattern of 'share and listen' that we described earlier. These groups may well choose to focus on helping people discern God's will for their lives.

Any of the above styles of small group may be suitable for those who are still coming to faith. Small groups have tremendous evangelistic potential in a postmodern world, especially those that adopt a spiritual direction approach. They can provide bridges over which spiritual seekers can pass into the exploration of the Christian faith. By being genuinely open to others, listening to their stories and engaging with them in their questions, we can provide a setting that enables the truth to be found. Spiritual mentoring allows for dialogue, honest searching and respect for individuals. It does not impose belief or demand a response; it seeks only to accompany on the journey. Thus it can provide a safe house for those who are curious about matters of faith but are afraid of entering a church. It can provide the welcome mat into a life of faith for the many spiritual seekers today.

How can this movement towards spiritual mentoring in small groups be integrated into church life? Larger churches may well be able to appoint a staff member who has special responsibility for spiritual formation. I have a friend in Singapore who does just this —her role is to encourage the church's small groups to have time for retreats and quiet days, and she also facilitates this for the church staff. She is available to train people in spiritual mentoring and can offer this on an individual basis, too. Such churches can easily set aside some of their small groups for the specific purpose of mentoring and could also provide support groups for the 'wanderers' we have mentioned.

Medium-sized churches may not be able to allocate a staff member for this work, but they may be able to encourage lay people to train in spiritual mentoring and to be available to the congregation. Perhaps once a month small groups could have a focus on spiritual direction, with leaders trained to help members listen together for God's voice. Even in smaller churches with fewer resources, there is no reason why one small group could not be set aside for this purpose. The leaders themselves could take training in mentoring and incorporate it into their pastoral care ministry.

Whatever the size of the congregation, those who preach can bear in mind that our ultimate goal is to help people discover their true identity in Christ, enjoy intimacy with God and find their own unique calling as they respond to God's will. If we consider not just how to explain God's word but also how to apply it strategically to our hearers, preaching itself can become a form of spiritual direction. Congregations will be healthier, more vibrant and see greater effectiveness as a result.

❖

—— *Chapter Thirteen* ——

Resting places:
Mentoring through retreats and quiet days

A sign commonly seen on British motorways gives a stark warning: 'Tiredness kills. Take a break.' It is a proven fact that drowsiness is the cause of many accidents on the road. People simply fall asleep at the wheel through exhaustion. On a long journey it is advisable to stop and have a rest. If we want to arrive safely at our destination, we need to plan time to recuperate on the way so that we can be refreshed. The same is true of our spiritual journey.

There is one particular passage in THE MESSAGE which has struck a chord with many people today. The words are those of Jesus in Matthew 11:28–30, and Peterson's gripping translation makes the familiar passage ring with contemporary relevance:

Are you tired? Worn out? Burned out on religion? Come to me. Get away with me and you'll recover your life. I'll show you how to take a real rest. Walk with me and work with me—watch how I do it. Learn the unforced rhythms of grace. I won't lay anything heavy or ill-fitting on you. Keep company with me and you'll learn to live freely and lightly.

I think the reason this particular passage has become so appreciated is because it resonates deeply with many of us. Yes, we are tired, and we do feel worn out. And we know that religious activism is in danger of burning us out. So when we hear the invitation of Jesus to get away for a rest in order to recover our lives we want to respond.

We yearn desperately to learn the unforced rhythms of grace and discover what it is to live freely and lightly. What was once seen as the greatest gospel promise for unbelievers is now regarded as the most wonderfully refreshing invitation to travel-weary pilgrims!

Hand in hand with the current upsurge of interest in spiritual mentoring is the dramatic increase in popularity of quiet days and retreats. The two are closely connected, of course, for spiritual mentoring is essentially about making the words of Jesus in the passage above alive and real to people, and it is in the context of 'time away' that the best mentoring takes place. In this chapter, therefore, we want to explore how leading people on quiet days and helping them on retreats can enhance the work of spiritual mentoring.

There is great value in stepping aside from our normal routine, even for a day, in order to focus on our relationship with God. Often in the course of a normal week we will have little time for reflection, little opportunity to stop and think where our life is going and what is happening to us. We simply keep living and responding to the next thing that comes along. If we are to become deeper people we will consciously have to create 'sacred space' for ourselves.

Distance gives us a sense of perspective. When we step back from the intensity of daily life we can often see a situation more clearly. Getting away can help us look at problems and issues more objectively, to regain perspective. It was James Irwin, the American astronaut, who said that the earth looks a tiny place when you see it from the moon. What seems so important to us close up can in fact look an awful lot smaller when we step back. Simply being in different surroundings can break our self-absorption and lift our spirits, putting us in a better place to hear God speak.

Taking time to rest is another vital reason for choosing to retreat for a while. It is not that we are running away from responsibility or becoming idle and self-indulgent. We all need time for ourselves, when we can be refreshed and renewed. John Chrysostom, one of the early Church Fathers, said that the bow which is never unstrung will quickly break. We cannot keep on working because we are not machines; we were made with the need to rest at least one day in seven. These are the maker's instructions, and life works better when we follow them and end up feeling rested, not exhausted. Neither were we made to keep on giving out to other people, for we do not have a limitless source of either energy or compassion. We need to take in refreshment for ourselves, and then we can give out to others. Soul care is the way we look after ourselves, so that we may continue to be available to others. 'Come with me by yourselves to a quiet place and get some rest' (Mark 6:31) is still the call of Jesus to careworn disciples.

Slowing down and finding stillness is never easy, but it pays remarkable dividends in terms of spiritual formation. It is in silence that we hear what is going on inside ourselves. Noise and hurry constantly mask our true condition and only when we are truly still can we recognize our own need for healing and wholeness. Further, silence provides us with a setting that makes it easier to develop spiritual sensitivity. Cut off from the distractions of television, the Internet and mobile phones, we are better able to tune into the still, small voice of God. No wonder the Lord says, 'Be still, and know that I am God' (Psalm 46:10).

By providing the opportunity for mentorees to have a quiet day or retreat, we will already have helped them on their way. Simply helping them to create 'soul space' will have benefited them already, for the reasons outlined above. But a quiet day or a retreat will give us as mentors the opportunity to take matters further and to do some real 'inner' soul work that may not be possible in the rush of everyday life.

A quiet day is the basic unit of retreat, and the term means exactly what it says—a day to be quiet. We can use a morning or an evening if we are hard pressed for time, but a full day will give us that much more space to unwind, relax and come to the point where we can readily engage with God. A day is not too long for most people to spend by themselves in prayer, reading, worship and reflection. It will also provide an opportunity for rest and for healthy exercise like walking. If we can enjoy such a day in the company of a spiritual mentor, so much the better. They will be able to advise how to use the time, and be available to listen if we want to talk things through. Some retreat centres organize quiet days which are led by an appropriately gifted speaker, and this more structured approach will appeal to some people. There will normally be a minimum of content, and what there is will point people in the right direction for their individual time with God.

Helpful as quiet days are, from my perspective there is nothing as beneficial as a residential retreat when it comes to helping people to grow spiritually. There are now retreat centres in many parts of the world, often in beautiful settings where it is easy to find peace and quiet, and where a spiritual atmosphere has been built up over generations of prayer and worship. A few days away gives more time for people to unwind and become physically rested, so that they can be more responsive to God. An extended period of time enables them to concentrate without interruption on what God may be saying or doing in their lives. It always amazes me how much ground can be covered in just a few short days away.

There are two main ways in which we can combine spiritual mentoring with a retreat. The first is what is often called an *individually guided retreat*. Here a mentor will work one-to-one with a mentoree in an approach that is tailor-made for the individual. The two will usually meet twice a day, in the morning and again in late afternoon or evening. The first session will probably involve listening to the mentoree, and then the mentor might suggest scripture for reflection or perhaps give some spiritual exercise similar to those in Appendix A. Further sessions will then be built around the issues arising out of that first time together. The process will unfold like a journey of its own. Neither person will know fully where it will take them; both will seek to be open to the Spirit's leading.

I recently led a group of three people on individually guided retreats at a retreat house in the beautiful Oxfordshire countryside. We began with a time together, when I shared with them a brief message from an appropriate passage of scripture and made some practical suggestions as to how they could best use the time. I then met with each of them individually twice a day for the period we were together, when I sought to respond to their particular concerns. Each followed their own pathway throughout the retreat, taking time to think and pray, to walk, rest and simply enjoy being away from their normal responsibilities. We met in the morning and evening together for prayers, but this was fairly brief and involved a simple, Christ-centred liturgy from the Northumbria Community.[1] I find it helpful to provide a basic rhythm for each day, a structure around which people can work. I have known all three people for some time, and they each hold responsible positions in local churches, but in different parts of the country, so meeting together in a central location and in a conducive setting gave me the opportunity to do further work with each of them.

The second way of combining spiritual mentoring and retreat is by means of a *led or preached retreat*. This is particularly appropriate for those who are just beginning on this pathway, for those who enjoy being with others and for those from a scripture-based church tradition. Normally there is an overall theme and spiritual input from the retreat leader, interspersed with reflective worship, personal time alone with God and, if appropriate, individual time with the leader. Retreats like this may be held in complete silence or, more commonly, use silence for designated periods. Group size can vary from a handful of people to as many as 30. Obviously, the larger the group the less personal it becomes.

I have sometimes led retreats based around Psalm 23.[2] This is a wonderful passage to use as a basis not only for teaching but also for spiritual guidance. It begins with establishing a very personal relationship with God (the Lord is *my* Shepherd) and the confidence we have as a result. Reflecting on the state of our personal relationship with God and our understanding of him is always a good place to begin a time of retreat. From there the psalmist takes us through three of the most common aspects of discipleship: learning to rest (vv. 2–3), learning to trust (vv. 3–4), and learning to live from divine resources (vv. 5–6). Each of these themes is rich in relevance to personal spiritual growth and can be taken as the theme for each day. The talks themselves can bring spiritual direction to the retreatants, as well as being the catalyst that will raise questions or provide the setting for them to share authentically about their own journeys with their mentor.

Another favourite passage of mine for use on retreat is John 15:1–17, the allegory of the vine and the branches.[3] Again, it is rich in suitable themes: Jesus as the true vine; the believer's union with him; how God works in our lives through cleansing and pruning; what it means to abide in Christ; how we learn the key lesson that 'apart from me you can do nothing' (v. 5); some of the key outcomes of abiding in Christ. Such a passage can become the basis for many personal conversations about our own faith journeys and what God is presently doing in our lives.

I have found that reflective worship is a key ingredient in a retreat setting. It allows us to reflect on the words used and can bring us closer to God. There is obviously a time for vibrant praise and worship, but in the context of a retreat quieter songs, which point to Jesus, work better. I often use a CD player, and people are invited either to listen to the songs or to join in with them if they wish. I find that instrumental music can also be powerfully used by the Spirit to bring a sense of stillness and the presence of God. It is perhaps another indication of what the Spirit is doing in these days that there seems to be a growing amount of excellent worship material available. As a mentor leading retreats you will want to create your own collection of songs that touch people's hearts and help to bring them into the presence of God.

I also encourage people to take time to journal while on retreat. This simple spiritual discipline involves writing down our deepest thoughts and feelings about our relationship with God and the journey we are taking. Journalling enables us to be very honest, and this is wonderfully cathartic in itself. It brings a sense of objectivity and clarity to our thinking and is a way of distinguishing what is real and what is false, thus discerning God's will for ourselves. It can also serve as a reminder of key things God has said to us or of answers to prayers and ways that God has worked in our lives. People will often then share from their journals in the individual mentoring times. Somehow it prepares their hearts and opens the way for the Spirit to bring further enlightenment.

Many years ago a friend said to me that 'time with God is always time well spent'. This has certainly been my experience, especially on retreat. We all need resting places on our journey, and time taken out of our busy schedules to be with God will bring its own reward. Mentors and mentorees both alike will find benefit from 'soul space'.

❖

--- *Chapter Fourteen* ---

Are we nearly there yet?
The goals of spiritual mentoring

Anyone who has travelled any distance with children will have been asked this question, and have been asked it repeatedly throughout the journey. 'Are we nearly there yet?' seems to be something of a universal cry among children about 20 minutes into any trip. Long journeys can be both tiring and boring for little people, who are always eager to arrive at their destination as quickly as possible.

In the spiritual life the journey is as important as the destination. What happens along the way really matters, and it is God's intention that we enjoy the journey we are on. Spiritual growth is a matter of process, and it cannot be rushed. We are to savour each moment, becoming alive and alert to what God is doing, responding to the movement of the Spirit in our hearts as he graciously invites us into deeper fellowship with the Son. There is no reason for us to be bored as we journey, for each new day is filled with adventure as we become more aware of his presence and more attuned to his voice. At the same time, the journey is taking us somewhere, and we must not forget our destination, otherwise we may end up going round in circles.

We have already spelled out in Chapter 2 some of the key goals of spiritual mentoring: to help people develop a growing intimacy with God; to discover their true identity as God's beloved children; to enter into their unique role of service within the kingdom of God. Expressed in terms of spiritual formation, our goal is to become like Christ. We desire his life to be formed within us. These are important aims, which we need to keep in mind throughout the mentoring relationship. I want to look in more detail now at how this works in practice and to point out the natural flow of growth and development that takes place on the journey.

As I have sought to live the Christian life myself and observed the lives of others on the same pathway, I have come to the conclusion that there are four key aspects in this journey to spiritual maturity. The starting point is a true experience of *grace*, which then leads to a place of *intimacy* with God. Once we have known what it is to be close to God we want to stay there and thus we learn to *abide* in Christ. Abiding in Christ then inevitably leads to *fruitfulness* of life, which is the true indicator of spiritual maturity.

Grace

So much has been written, sung and spoken about grace in recent years that we are in danger of making the word seem threadbare, of rendering it meaningless by overuse. Yet for those who experience grace in their lives, it remains 'wonderful', 'amazing', even 'outrageous', and words would never be adequate to describe the effect it has on us.

Grace is often simply defined as 'the unmerited favour of God', but a one-sentence definition can never properly convey all that is contained and offered to us in this most beautiful of words. The Bible uses the term 'grace' to describe the activity of a loving God towards a needy world and, like a sparkling diamond, it has many facets, depending on the light and how you look at it. Grace and mercy go hand in hand, for while grace describes the activity of God, mercy describes his attitude, which in some ways comes first. It is because God is merciful (not giving us what we do deserve—judgment) that he can then be gracious (giving us what we don't deserve—favour and blessing).

My first conscious encounter with grace came when I realized that God really does love me unconditionally. This discovery marked a major spiritual breakthrough for me, for until this point I had lived as so many people do, thinking that I had to earn God's approval through my performance. Not having a very good opinion of myself, I struggled to think that a holy God could do anything but frown upon me. When I realized that God loves us because it is his nature to love, and that his love for me is dependent upon his unchanging character and not upon my faultless behaviour, I began to relax and to rest in his acceptance of me. It is vital that the truth of 1 John 4:19 is established in the heart of all those who follow Jesus: 'We love because he first loved us.' Our love is at best a response to the prior love of God. What counts is not our hold on God but his hold on us.

Grace reminds us that the initiative is always with God, and this is at the heart of our salvation. We were dead in our sins and unable to save ourselves. God, who is rich in mercy and full of love towards us, acted to save us so that we can now know forgiveness and eternal life. We could neither earn this nor do we deserve it. It comes to us purely as a gift and by the initiative of God: 'For it is by grace you have been saved, through faith—and this not from yourselves, it is the gift of God—not by works, so that no one can boast' (Ephesians 2:8). Here we see a pattern that holds good for the whole of the Christian life. God is always the first mover, and we respond to what he has already begun. Grace (God's initiative) is followed by faith (our grateful response). Once this principle has been established in our hearts, it sets us free from striving to do God's will in our own strength, and from thinking that everything depends upon us.

It is in this sense that grace is the opposite of law. Once we realize that we are justified freely by God's grace and not by keeping the law (Romans 3:22–24), we can be released from the curse of legalism. By 'legalism' we mean all the ways by which we try to earn God's favour by keeping religious rules—whether our own or those imposed on us by others. It is endemic in most churches, and it cripples spiritual growth and vitality. In some ways I 'fell into' grace, because for many years I was part of such a legalistic system. Only when I saw how much we had added to the gospel of grace by our religious demands, did I discover the true freedom in Christ (Galatians 5:1).

Many of those we mentor will be crippled by legalism, either because they have imposed rules upon themselves, or because they are part of legalistic systems. This results either in self-righteousness (because we kept the rules and are therefore better than others) or self-condemnation (because we didn't keep the rules and are therefore worse than others). These are the 'infectious diseases' of the Christian life, and only a true understanding of grace can set us free from their damaging and limiting effects.

Grace not only gets us going in the Christian life, but it also sustains us along the way. 'Just as you received Christ Jesus as Lord,' says the apostle Paul, 'continue to live in him' (Colossians 2:6). It is grace that equips us for the tasks of mission and ministry. God imparts gifts to us (both natural and spiritual) by which we can serve him effectively. As we identify and use these gifts, we begin to be used by God. 'We have different gifts,' says Paul, 'according to the grace given us' (Romans 12:6). Spiritual mentoring will involve helping others not only to discover their gifts but to have the confidence to use them. And the awareness that our gifts are God-given helps us keep our feet on the ground and remain humble throughout.

The flow of God's grace continues towards us with every new call to obedience and every new step along the path of discipleship, for whatever God asks us to do, he enables us to do. In this sense God's commands are always his promises, because whatever challenge lies before us, it carries with it a divine enabling. Paul's own apostolic ministry was built around this experience: 'But by the grace of God I am what I am, and his grace toward me was not without effect. No, I worked harder than all of them—yet not I, but the grace of God that was with me' (1 Corinthians 15:10).

In the awareness of God's grace, it will be our joy to stand with people in the midst of the trials and tribulations that life will inevitably bring along, for grace is nothing less than God's strength in our weakness. Faced with insurmountable difficulties and stretched on every side, we can nevertheless receive an even deeper inflow of grace, for that is when we hear the divine whisper, 'My grace is sufficient for you' (2 Corinthians 12:9–10). It is then that we can experience one of the great paradoxes of the Christian life—that when we are weak, then we are strong, for the power of Christ rests upon us in our weakness.

Intimacy

Once we have discovered that God is a God of grace, we will be free to approach him with confidence and begin to enter a life of intimacy and fellowship with him. As long as we think of God as being harsh, critical and demanding, we will not want to come near—indeed, we will want to hide ourselves away out of fear of disappointing or offending him. At best we will approach God in our 'Sunday best', showing only our presentable side to him and trying to create a front of acceptability. Once we realize that God loves us unconditionally, we will be liberated to come to him as we are, in the complete abandonment and childlike joy of those who know they are truly loved. Only then can we live before God in a way that is natural and authentic.

The invitation to intimacy with God may sound grand but it is one of the reasons why Jesus died on the cross—to reconcile us to God and bring us back into a personal relationship with him. Those who were once far away have now been brought near (Ephesians 2:13). We who were excluded from his presence now have access to God (Romans 5:1–2). We can once more enjoy the kind of fellowship that Adam and Eve enjoyed in the garden of Eden— walking and talking with God in the cool of the day. This is the privilege of every redeemed child of God.

The word 'intimacy' suggests closeness, oneness and together-ness, and these are all good words to describe what we mean by the devotional life. Prayer and worship are the main expressions of intimacy with God. Prayer is essentially about communion with God and, as we have noted already, one of the challenges for a mentor will be to help others enter into a deeper, richer and more meaningful prayer life. Most Christians struggle with prayer and most probably wish they had a better prayer life. Prayer has many expressions—confession, thanksgiving, praise, supplication, intercession and so on—but intimacy with God is best developed within the context of contemplative prayer. Once we get beyond the need to be always talking or having a set agenda in prayer, we are free to discover the joy of simply being with God and of listening to what he might want to say to us. In this setting the intimacy of com-munion can take place, a closeness which does not need words and where silence is the contentment of lovers.

One of the Greek words for 'worship' is *proskuneo*, which literally means 'to blow a kiss'. Worship, either with others or alone, provides another setting for intimacy with God, and in particular for the discovery of our own belovedness. Here we can not only speak of our love for God but also allow him, through the ministry of the Holy Spirit, to reveal his love for us (Romans 5:5). Finding our identity as God's beloved children is essential to building a healthy spiritual life. Brennan Manning, one of my favourite writers on the inner life, puts this truth so well. 'Define yourself radically as one beloved by God,' he says. 'This is the true self. All other identity is illusion.'[1] In many ways the journey of the Christian life is a journey into the love of God, and into the recognition that this simple truth is the heart of the matter.

Christians around the world are hearing a fresh call to intimacy with God and are feeling a longing for living deeper. It can best be summed up as an invitation to the church from the Divine Lover, as in the words from the Song of Songs: 'Arise, my darling, my beautiful one, and come with me' (2:10). Intimacy at any level can only be developed by spending quality time together and, while this is so obviously true of the spiritual dimension, it is one of the things we find most difficult to do. The greatest barrier to intimacy is our busyness and our inability to be still on the inside. This is why the classic spiritual disciplines of stillness, silence and solitude need to be rediscovered and taught to a new generation. The current renewed interest in retreats, quiet days and the use of spiritual exercises is an encouraging development. Mentors can take hold of this and encourage those they seek to help to take time out to develop their relationship with God.

Abiding

Once people discover the joy of intimacy with God and the delights of his presence, they want to stay there. The next challenge is learning how to abide in Christ and make him our dwelling place and the source of our life. We do not want to flit in and out of God's presence but to live there continually. Of course this is not easy, especially with a fast-paced and demanding lifestyle, but it is possible, and this is exactly what Jesus spoke about in John 15. Using the allegory of the vine and the branches, Jesus shows us how it is possible to live in union with himself: 'I am the vine; you are the branches. If a man remains in me and I in him, he will bear much fruit; apart from me you can do nothing' (v. 5). Here we are reminded of two significant truths—that we are in Christ, and Christ is in us. The more we realize that this is the case, the more we will begin to share his risen life and allow him to live in us and through us. Christian living is not a matter of imitating Jesus in an external way but of participating in his life and allowing that life to be expressed through us.

One painful lesson is hinted at in what Jesus says here—that apart from him we can do nothing. Most of us have spent a good deal of time trying to do things without God, and we have developed ways and means of getting through life on our own, of being strong, resilient and self-sufficient. In his love and wisdom God gently has to dismantle some of these patterns of independent living until we come again to the place of dependency upon him that was his original intention for us. A wise mentor will recognize when this 'dismantling' is taking place in someone's life and help them to understand what God may be doing. It still remains a painful time, but knowing it has a good purpose can help us through and encourage us to yield ourselves more willingly to God.

Just as the branch draws its life from the vine, so we are to draw spiritual strength and nourishment from Jesus. Experiences of weakness, failure and brokenness prepare us for this; practice of the spiritual disciplines enables us to do it, following the 'holy habits' which help us to access the grace of God. We have already mentioned stillness, silence and solitude. They also include prayer, fellowship, teaching and breaking bread (Acts 2:42), as well as fasting, confession, worship, giving and service. We can add to this list the disciplines of reflection and self-examination, together with Bible study and meditation, awareness of God in the world around us, and attunement to the Spirit. This is not an exhaustive list nor is it meant to push us back into legalism. We use the disciplines in so far as they are helpful and appropriate, and only as a means to an end—that through them we might encounter the risen Christ and receive his life into us afresh.

Fruitfulness

Abiding helps us to become centred on God and dependent on the life of Christ within us. Once we do this something amazing happens, and it happens naturally and without significant effort on our part: we begin to bear fruit. Our lives then begin to impact the lives of others for good. When a tree bears fruit we can say that it is mature, and when a person's life begins to produce spiritual fruit, it is a sign that they are coming to maturity in Christ.

What do we mean by fruit? It is the outward expression of the life of God within. In other words, if I have the life of Jesus within me, it will inevitably express itself in my thoughts, words and actions and I will reveal the fruit of the Spirit as itemized in Galatians 5:22. It may show itself in heartfelt worship to God or in sensitively sharing the gospel with those who have not heard it. It will be there in the carefulness of my words or the integrity of my decision-making. No part of my life will be unaffected.

It is God's will that each of us should live a fruitful life. This is what Jesus meant when he said, 'You did not choose me, but I chose you and appointed you to go and bear fruit—fruit that will last' (John 15:16). God has a plan and purpose for each of us, and mentoring is about helping individuals to discover that plan. It involves resourcing them to identify their own unique calling and gifting and then helping them learn how to live their life in God so that they become fruitful as they fulfil that calling.

These are the four key aspects of spiritual growth as I see it, and they form the framework for my own work of spiritual mentoring. I am constantly looking at my own life from this perspective, and as I seek to help others I use it as a reference point, asking such questions as these:

- Where is this person in their experience of grace?
- How can I help them to discover their 'belovedness'?
- What will help them to discover their identity 'in Christ' and become more aware of the Christ who is within them?
- How is God at work in their life to produce the fruit of the Spirit and glorify him through their life and service?
- Is 'brokenness' an issue? How is God revealing this person's weakness to them, thus creating the dependency through which he can work?

In doing this I am not trying to squeeze people into my own mould or to make clones out of them; I am simply trying to follow my understanding of the Christian way as it has been shown to me. We can only lead others where we ourselves have been. We can only journey together if we are going in the same direction.

⁕

———— *Appendix A* ————

Spiritual exercises

Here are a few examples of the kind of 'exercise' that can be used in the context of spiritual mentoring. The aim of such exercises is to provide practical ways for people to reflect on their relationship with God.

Exercise 1: your relationship with God

Draw a picture or diagram to describe your relationship with God at this time, being as honest as you can. We are not looking for a great work of art but something that allows you to express what is in your heart.

Now draw a second picture or diagram to show what you would like your relationship with God to be like.

Notice the difference between the two diagrams. How do you account for the gap between the reality and what might be? Think about this for a while. What are the factors in your life that work against a closer relationship with God?

Write a simple prayer that expresses your longing to move from the first diagram to the second.

What action can you take that will work towards a closer relationship with God?

Exercise 2: an awareness walk

Go for a very leisurely walk outside or just find somewhere comfortable outdoors to sit. Use all five senses to engage with the world which God the Creator has made. Remember Psalm 8:3–4: 'When I consider your heavens... what is man?' and the words of Jesus: 'Look at the birds... see... the lilies' (Matthew 6:26, 28).

Seek to become aware of God in the world around you.

Now *look*... What can you *see*? A bird, a beetle, a worm, a spider's web?

Look at the grasses—many different kinds... *touch* them... look carefully at them... Also the leaves and twigs and bark...

Look at the flowers... touch them gently so that you do not harm them... Look at the leaves, the blossoms... *Smell* their fragrance.

Now *listen*... you may hear cars but what else can you hear—a bird? The rustling of leaves? The chirrup of an insect?

Perhaps there is something you can *taste*?

Now look at the larger scene: the great trees... the patterns in the clouds... the colours of the sky... use your intuition to ponder the meaning of it all. Become attentive to the God who is present in the natural world around you.

Be alert to whatever grabs your attention, which 'accidentally' come across your path. Recognize that God is in such happenings. How might they speak to you?

And all this—made by God. Worship him who made all this.

'What is man?' Who am I? And yet I am loved and 'the very hairs of [my] head' (Matthew 10:30) are known to him.

Allow your heart to rise to God in worship and praise.

Perhaps collect a few items without spoiling the garden or the countryside to take back to make a small display.

Exercise 3: developing a timeline

Take a piece of paper and draw a line down the middle from top to bottom. This represents the span of your life from birth to the present and onwards.

a) Mark off the line into sections of five or ten years. You can put the years on as well.
b) Now to the left of the line, begin to mark the significant moments in your life: starting school, going to university, getting a job, getting married, and so on.
c) On the right, identify the key moments of your spiritual experience.
d) On either side of the line, try to identify times of particular challenge for you. Identify your feelings at those times if possible.
e) Reflect on the whole diagram. Add anything else that comes to mind as being relevant. What are the ways God has been shaping you through your life experiences? What are the key lessons of your life?
f) Look ahead from where you are now. How can your past be used positively in your future? How might what has happened to you be incorporated into future ministry?

Exercise 4: the prayer of examen or prayer of review

Think back over the last 24 hours or, if you prefer, the last two to three days. Replay the events in your mind, like a video recording. Try to do this in chronological order. You may need to go over this several times and make simple notes of all that took place.

Where can you discern the activity of God in your life during this period?

Were there moments when you were led by God?

... when you heard the prompting of his Spirit?

... when you were conscious of God's presence, or moved to worship?

Can you see evidence of God's provision? Of his protection? Of his goodness?

Give thanks for his working in you.

Can you identify occasions when God was working through you?

... when you produced the fruit of the Spirit? Love, joy, peace, patience...

... when you did something that was an expression of your faith?

... when you were able to share your faith with another person?

... when you were moved to pray?

... when you felt the pull of temptation, but by God's grace resisted?

Give thanks for his working in you.

Are you aware of moments when you may have made mistakes, or sinned?

Is there anything that you regret?

Did you miss opportunities to live out your faith?

Were there times when you became anxious, worried or afraid?

What difficulties did you encounter? What problems emerged?

When was God calling you to trust him?

Give thanks for his working in you, for his forgiveness and nearness in times of trouble.

Is there anything that you would like to do tomorrow (or in the near future) as a result of this review of your life? Bring it before God and ask him for the grace to turn desire into action.

Exercise 5: energy review

How would you evaluate your energy level at present?

There is a significant link between the amount of energy we have and our spiritual life. Of course God can, and does, use us when we are 'weak' (physically drained), but when we feel tired and exhausted most of the time it is harder to apprehend God's presence, more difficult to concentrate on prayer and Bible study, and more of an effort to give ourselves in worship or service. Are there any words that describe how you feel energy-wise at the moment?

Are you running on empty? It may be helpful to compare the amount of energy you feel you have to the amount of fuel in the tank of a car. What would the gauge be reading?

Empty	You are stalled at the roadside and can go no further.
In the red	You are just about coping, but can't take much more.
1/4 full	You have a little energy, but feel below par.
1/2 full	You are OK but are aware you have given out a lot.
3/4 full	You are functioning as normal.
Full	You are bursting with life and vitality, raring to go!

When we realize we are running on empty, it is time to stop and refuel. We cannot go on and on giving out without stopping to receive ourselves. Even Jesus was aware that 'virtue' went out from him (see Mark 5:30).

What has 'drained' you of energy?

What is giving energy to you?

How can you refuel yourself?

A promise from God: The Lord is the everlasting God, the Creator of the ends of the earth. He will not grow tired or weary, and his understanding no one can fathom. He gives strength to the weary and increases the power of the weak. Even youths grow tired and weary, and young men stumble and fall; but those who hope in the Lord will renew their strength. They will soar on wings like eagles; they will run and not grow weary, they will walk and not be faint (Isaiah 40:28–31).

—————— *Appendix B* ——————

Contemplative Bible reading
or *Lectio Divina*

Lectio Divina is an ancient method of Bible reading, with the aim of helping us to hear God speak to us personally. It was introduced by St Benedict for the benefit of those who followed his Rule, and is currently coming back into popularity. Rather than being about studying the Bible, it is a way of simply allowing the scriptures to speak to us. Choose a fairly short passage with lots of descriptive words, which is not too doctrinally based. The Psalms and Gospels are ideal for this purpose. Suitable passages to start with might be Song of Songs 2:14–15, Isaiah 43:1–2, Matthew 3:16–17, Mark 6:30–32.

1. **Prepare by quieting yourself and letting your body relax.** Sit comfortably, alert, maybe with your eyes closed, and centre yourself with breathing slowly. Pray that God will speak to you, and ask for 'ears to hear'.
2. **Hear the word (that is addressed to you).** As the passage is read twice, listen for the word or phrase that strikes you or attracts you. Don't try to understand it or to fathom it, but simply receive the word(s) given to you. During the silence repeat it to yourself softly or silently. When the leader invites you, say aloud only that word or phrase, without elaboration or explanation.
3. **Ask, 'How is my life touched by this word?'** The passage is read again. Listen to discover how this word connects with your life. What is God saying to you through it? Be prepared for any image

or picture that comes to mind. Again, simply receive what is given to you and in the silence meditate on it. When invited, and if you wish to do so, share in one or two sentences how you feel the word connects with your life.

4. **Ask, 'Is there an invitation for me to respond to?'** After the passage is read a third time, ponder what response you should make. Is there something God wants you to be? Is there something he wants you to do? What is his invitation to you through the word he has given you? When invited, share briefly your response, if you wish to do so. Listen to the other group members, especially the person on your right.

5. **Pray for one another to be able to respond.** Pray briefly for the person on your right, either aloud or quietly, that God will help them to respond.

Further reading

Richard Peace, *Contemplative Bible Reading*, Nav Press, 1998
Norvene Vest, *Knowing by Heart*, DLT, 1993

—————— *Appendix C* ——————

Ethical guidelines for spiritual mentoring

These guidelines are an extract from the guidelines published by Spiritual Directors International and are used by permission.

Covenant

1. Spiritual directors initiate conversation and establish agreements with directees about:
   a) the nature of spiritual direction
   b) the roles of the director and directee
   c) the length and frequency of direction sessions
   d) the compensation, if any, to be given to the director or institution
   e) the process for evaluating and terminating the friendship.

Dignity

2. Spiritual directors honour the dignity of the directee by:
   a) respecting the directee's values, conscience, spirituality and theology
   b) inquiring into the motives, experiences or relationships of the directee only as necessary
   c) recognizing the imbalance of power in the spiritual direction relationship and taking care not to exploit it
   d) establishing and maintaining appropriate physical and psychological boundaries with the directee

e) refraining from sexualized behaviour, including, but not limited to, manipulative, abusive or coercive words or actions towards a directee.

Confidentiality

3. Spiritual directors maintain the confidentiality and the privacy of the directee by:
   a) protecting the identity of the directee
   b) keeping confidential all oral and written matters arising in the spiritual direction sessions
   c) conducting direction sessions in appropriate settings
   d) addressing legal regulations requiring disclosure to proper authorities, including but not limited to, child abuse, elder abuse and physical harm to self and others.

For more information, contact Spiritual Directors International, PO Box 3584, Bellevue, WA 98009-3584, USA.
Website: www.sdiworld.org.

BIBLIOGRAPHY

Keith Anderson and Randy Reese, *Spiritual Mentoring*, Eagle, 1999

Howard Baker, *Soul Keeping*, NavPress, 1998

Peter Ball, *Introducing Spiritual Direction*, SPCK, 2003

Jeanette Bakke, *Holy Invitations*, Baker Books, 2000

David Benner, *Sacred Companions*, IVP, 2002

Annice Callahan, *Spiritual Guides for Today*, DLT, 1992

Maureen Conroy, *Looking into the Well*, Loyola Press, 1995

Larry Crabb, *Soul Talk*, Integrity, 2003

Bruce Demarest, *Satisfy Your Soul*, NavPress, 1999

Bruce Demarest, *Soul Guide*, NavPress, 2003

Rose Mary Dougherty, *Group Spiritual Direction*, Paulist Press, 1995

Tilden Edwards, *Spiritual Friend*, Paulist Press, 1980

Margaret Guenther, *Holy Listening*, Cowley Press, 1992

Kenneth Leech, *Soul Friend*, Sheldon Press, 1977

Anne Long, *Approaches to Spiritual Direction*, Grove Books, 1984

Thomas Merton, *Spiritual Direction and Meditation*, Anthony Clarke, 1975

Gary Moon and David Benner, *Spiritual Direction and the Care of Souls*, Eagle, 2005

Robert Mulholland, *Invitation to a Journey*, IVP, 1993

Henri Nouwen, *Spiritual Direction*, Harper San Francisco, 2006

Eugene Peterson, *The Wisdom of Each Other*, Zondervan, 1998

Janet Ruffing, *Spiritual Direction*, Paulist Press, 2000

Ray Simpson, *Soul Friendship*, Hodder & Stoughton, 1999

Edward Sellner, *Mentoring*, Cowley Press, 2002

Jean Stairs, *Listening for the Soul*, Fortress Press, 2000

Martin Thornton, *Spiritual Direction*, SPCK, 1984

Norvene Vest (ed.), *Tending the Holy,* Continuum, 2004

Heather Webb, *Small Group Leadership as Spiritual Direction,* Zondervan, 2005

❖

NOTES

Introduction

1 Larry Crabb in his foreword to David Benner, *Sacred Companions*, IVP, 2002, pp. 9–10.

2 Selwyn Hughes, *My Story*, CWR, 2004, p. 378.

3 Rob Frost, *Five Things I Wish They'd Told Me When I Became a Christian*, Authentic, 2006, p. 108.

Chapter 1: Point of departure: What exactly is spiritual mentoring?

1 Eugene Peterson, *Working the Angles*, Eerdmans, 1987, p. 103.

2 John Mallison, *Mentoring to Develop Disciples and Leaders*, Scripture Union, 1999, p. 8.

3 Bruce Demarest, *Satisfy Your Soul*, NavPress, 1999, p. 193.

4 David Benner, *Sacred Companions*, IVP, 2004, p. 94.

5 Keith Anderson and Randy Reese, *Spiritual Mentoring*, Eagle, 1999, p. 12.

6 Benner, *Sacred Companions*, p. 87.

Chapter 2: Ready for adventure: The philosophy behind spiritual mentoring

1 Anderson and Reese, *Spiritual Mentoring*, p. 50.

2 Benner, *Sacred Companions*, p. 108.

3 Howard Baker, *Soul Keeping*, NavPress, 1998, pp. 33–37.

Chapter 3: Ancient paths: spiritual mentoring in the Bible and church history

1 Bruce Demarest, *Soul Guide*, NavPress, 2003, p. 15.

2 Aelred of Rievaulx, quoted by Anderson and Reese, *Spiritual Mentoring*, p. 86.

3 Quoted by Bruce Demarest in *Soul Guide*, p. 49.

Chapter 4: Travelling companions: What it means to be a spiritual friend

1 Bryn Hughes, *Discipling, Coaching, Mentoring*, Kingsway, 2003, p. 79.
2 Benner, *Sacred Companions*, p. 57.

Chapter 5: Reliable guides: Qualities, skills and tools of a mentor

1 Anderson and Reese, *Spiritual Mentoring,* chapter 3.
2 Hughes, *Discipling, Coaching, Mentoring*, p. 109.
3 Margaret Silf, *Landmarks*, DLT, 1998.
4 Ray Simpson, *The Joy of Spiritual Fitness*, Zondervan, 2003.

Chapter 6: The scenic route: Developing spiritual awareness

1 Benner, *Sacred Companions*, p. 96.
2 Jean-Pierre de Caussade, *The Sacrament of the Present Moment*, Fount, 1981, p. 84.
3 John Ortberg, *God is Closer Than You Think*, Zondervan, 2005, pp. 67–68.
4 George Matheson, *O Love That Wilt Not Let Me Go*, 1882.

Chapter 7: A sense of direction: The gift of discernment

1 Anderson and Reese, *Spiritual Mentoring*, p. 167.
2 Stephen Bryant, 'What is Spiritual Discernment by Consensus?' in *Raising People to a Lifestyle*, Volume 2, Issue 1, p. 2.
3 Jeanette Bakke, *Holy Invitations*, Baker Books, 2000, p. 218.
4 Alex B. Aronis, *Developing Intimacy with God*, Union Church of Manila, 2002, p. 7.

Chapter 8: Road maps and guidebooks: Insights for busy mentors

1 See Robert Mulholland, *Invitation to a Journey*, IVP, 1993, pp. 79–101.
2 Dr J. Robert Clinton, *The Making of a Leader*, NavPress, 1988.

3 Janet Hagberg and Robert Guelich, *The Critical Journey*, Sheffield Publishing Company, 2005.
4 Hagberg and Guelich, *The Critical Journey*, p. 114.
5 Hagberg and Guelich, *The Critical Journey*, p. XXV.

Chapter 9: Roadside assistance: Some of the key issues
1 Peter Ball, *Introducing Spiritual Direction*, SPCK, 2003, p. 13.
2 See, for example, Gary Thomas, *Sacred Pathways*, Zondervan, 2000.
3 John Chapman, *Spiritual Letters*, re-issued by Burns & Oates, 2003.
4 For more on this, see Larry Crabb, *Shattered Dreams*, Waterbrook, 2001.
5 Alison Palmer, 'Issues Facing Returning Missionaries and how Spiritual Direction can Help', unpublished paper available on the Internet (www.sgm.org.nz/research_papers.htm).

Chapter 10: Losing the way: Mentoring those with questions of faith
1 Alan Jamieson, *A Churchless Faith*, SPCK, 2002.
2 Alan Jamieson, *Journeying Faith*, SPCK, 2004, chapter 2.
3 See, for example, Spirited Exchanges, www.spiritedexchanges.org.nz

Chapter 11: Travelling by night: When God seems absent
1 Gordon Mursell (ed.), *The Story of Christian Spirituality*, Lion Publishing, 2001, p. 210.
2 Russell Metcalfe, Internet article from www.wordaction.com
3 Alexander Ryrie, *Silent Waiting*, Canterbury Press, 1999, pp. 170–171.
4 Demarest, *Satisfy Your Soul*, p. 214.
5 Hagberg and Guelich, *The Critical Journey*, pp. 153–154.

Chapter 12: Group travel: Spiritual mentoring in small groups

1 Robert Bellah, *Habits of the Heart*, Winston-Seabury Press, 1982, p. 79.
2 Heather Webb, *Small Group Leadership as Spiritual Direction*, Zondervan, 2005, p. 24.
3 Benner, *Sacred Companions*, chapter 8.
4 Rose Mary Dougherty, *Group Spiritual Direction*, Paulist Press, 1995, p. 35.
5 Webb, *Small Group Leadership as Spiritual Direction*, p. 123.

Chapter 13: Resting places: Mentoring through retreats and quiet days

1 Available from the Northumbria Community, Cloisters, Hetton Hall, Chatton, Northumberland, NE66 5SD (www.northumbriacommunity.org).
2 See Tony Horsfall, *Song of the Shepherd*, BRF, 2002.
3 See Tony Horsfall, *A Fruitful Life*, BRF, 2004.

Chapter 14: Are we nearly there yet? The goals of spiritual mentoring

1 Brennan Manning, *Abba's Child*, NavPress, 1994, p. 59.